Nuclear Energy

by Kevin Hillstrom

LUCENT BOOKS
A part of Gale, Cengage Learning

GALE
CENGAGE Learning·

Detroit • New York • San Francisco • New Haven, Conn • Waterville, Maine • London

LIBRARY OF CONGRESS CATALOGING-IN-PUBLICATION DATA

Hillstrom, Kevin, 1963-
  Nuclear energy / by Kevin Hillstrom.
     pages cm. -- (Hot topics)
  Includes bibliographical references and index.
  Summary: "The books in this series objectively and thoughtfully explore topics of political, social, cultural, economic, moral, historical, or environmental importance"-- Provided by publisher.
  Includes bibliographical references and index.
  ISBN 978-1-4205-0874-1 (hardback)
  1. Nuclear energy--Juvenile literature. I. Title.
  TK9148.H55 2014
  333.792'4--dc23
                                                        2013022293

Lucent Books
27500 Drake Rd.
Farmington Hills, MI 48331

ISBN-13: 978-1-4205-0874-1
ISBN-10: 1-4205-0874-1

Printed in the United States of America
1 2 3 4 5 6 7 17 16 15 14 13

CONTENTS

FOREWORD

Young people today are bombarded with information. Aside from traditional sources such as newspapers, television, and the radio, they are inundated with a nearly continuous stream of data from electronic media. They send and receive e-mails and instant messages, read and write online "blogs," participate in chat rooms and forums, and surf the web for hours. This trend is likely to continue. As Patricia Senn Breivik, the former dean of university libraries at Wayne State University in Detroit, has stated, "Information overload will only increase in the future. By 2020, for example, the available body of information is expected to double every 73 days! How will these students find the information they need in this coming tidal wave of information?"

Ironically, this overabundance of information can actually impede efforts to understand complex issues. Whether the topic is abortion, the death penalty, gay rights, or obesity, the deluge of fact and opinion that floods the print and electronic media is overwhelming. The news media report the results of polls and studies that contradict one another. Cable news shows, talk radio programs, and newspaper editorials promote narrow viewpoints and omit facts that challenge their own political biases. The World Wide Web is an electronic minefield where legitimate scholars compete with the postings of ordinary citizens who may or may not be well-informed or capable of reasoned argument. At times, strongly worded testimonials and opinion pieces both in print and electronic media are presented as factual accounts.

Conflicting quotes and statistics can confuse even the most diligent researchers. A good example of this is the question of whether or not the death penalty deters crime. For instance, one study found that murders decreased by nearly one-third when the death penalty was reinstated in New York in 1995. Death penalty supporters cite this finding to support their argument that the existence of the death penalty deters criminals from committing murder. However, another study found that states without the death penalty have murder rates below the national average. This study is cited by opponents of capital punishment, who reject the claim that the death penalty deters murder. Students need context and clear, informed discussion if they are to think critically and make informed decisions.

The Hot Topics series is designed to help young people wade through the glut of fact, opinion, and rhetoric so that they can think critically about controversial issues. Only by reading and thinking critically will they be able to formulate a viewpoint that is not simply the parroted views of others. Each volume of the series focuses on one of today's most pressing social issues and provides a balanced overview of the topic. Carefully crafted narrative, fully documented primary and secondary source quotes, informative sidebars, and study questions all provide excellent starting points for research and discussion. Full-color photographs and charts enhance all volumes in the series. With its many useful features, the Hot Topics series is a valuable resource for young people struggling to understand the pressing issues of the modern era.

NUCLEAR POWER AND THE WORLD'S ENERGY FUTURE

As the United States and other nations around the world move ever deeper into the twenty-first century, they find themselves at an important developmental crossroad. Billions of the world's citizens now live daily lives of relative comfort and affluence, thanks to scientific and technological breakthroughs that have transformed every aspect of human existence. These breakthroughs range from vast electrical systems that power our televisions, lights, appliances, and furnaces to sophisticated vehicles capable of transporting people over land and water and through the air at speeds undreamed of one hundred years ago.

Meanwhile, billions of other people who do not yet have reliable electricity, clean water supplies, or modern transportation options are pushing to change their circumstances. Governments and corporations in China, India, and other fast-developing parts of the globe are investing heavily in innovative technologies and sleek new machines that are modernizing their economies and lifting millions out of poverty every year.

The positive aspects of these historical developments and recent trends have been shadowed by two questions that have been growing in intensity with each passing year. Where are the nations of the world going to find the energy to keep all their industrial machinery and technological marvels operating for centuries to come? And will their energy choices and consumption habits end up destroying the ecological health and vitality of the planet itself?

Nuclear power has been at the forefront of these discussions for more than half a century. Ever since it came on the scene in the post–World War II era, nuclear technology has been touted as a clean and potent energy source. These attributes have convinced many people that nuclear energy can free the world from its long-time dependence on fossil fuels like coal and oil, the burning of which generates greenhouse gases that contribute to global warming. But nuclear energy has also received strong opposition from people who say that the technology has too many drawbacks. Anti-nuclear protesters point out that accidents at nuclear facilities have caused deaths and environmental contamination of large swaths of land, and they charge that the financial expense of generating nuclear power is too great. Many critics of nuclear energy believe that the world should instead invest in so-called renewable energy resources like wind and solar power that can also combat global climate change. Both supporters and detractors of nuclear energy agree, though, that decisions about how it is used or whether it is used will go a long way toward determining the kind of world people will live in for centuries to come.

THE HISTORY OF NUCLEAR ENERGY

Over the last two centuries, humankind has turned its ever-growing scientific knowledge, bountiful natural resources, and mighty industrial machines to the task of producing energy for the world's needs. For much of that time, this energy has been pulled from the very elements of the earth and sky.

The most widely used energy sources are so-called fossil fuels. These resources—oil, coal, and natural gas—formed millions of years ago when ancient vegetation became squeezed under layers of sedimentary rock. Since the onset of the Industrial Revolution in the late eighteenth century, scientists and engineers have developed ingenious processes for bringing these fuels to the surface and using them to heat homes, light streets, and power trains, ships, planes, and automobiles. Oil, coal, and natural gas subsequently became the most valuable and heavily used energy sources on the planet. But the earth contains only a finite supply of these fossil fuels, and their consumption creates pollution and other serious environmental problems.

Scientists and engineers also have worked together to seek out alternatives to fossil fuels. In the late nineteenth century, they turned their attention to naturally flowing rivers, which had long been used to turn the great wheels of riverside grain and lumber mills. Researchers and builders learned how to install massive dams that take the energy contained in moving water and convert it into hydroelectricity (from *hydro*, the ancient Greek word for "water"). Hydropower transformed rivers in some parts of the world into major energy sources. Critics, however, have long claimed that hydroelectric dams do too much damage to natural areas and fish migrations. They also point out that hydroelectricity will never match the importance of fossil fuels because the earth contains only a limited number of major rivers that can be dammed.

Finally, scientists have labored for decades to harness forces high above the earth's surface to meet our energy needs. They have built mighty wind turbines that create usable energy out of the winds that race across the planet. They have also developed solar panels and solar batteries to harness the power of the sun and create electricity. But neither of these so-called renewable energy sources accounts for more than a fraction of the total energy production of the United States and other industrialized nations. Even in Denmark, which gets a higher percentage of its total energy production from wind power than any other country, wind power accounts for only about 25 percent of the nation's total energy needs.

As an early alternative to fossil fuels, massive dams such as this one were built to harness the power of moving water to produce electricity.

Seeking Out the Secrets of the Atom

The final piece of the energy puzzle in the modern world is nuclear power, which has been the subject of both intense praise and heated condemnation since it emerged into public view in the 1940s. Nuclear power is based on manipulation of atoms, the building blocks of all matter in the universe. Ancient Greek philosophers were the first people to propose that all of the physical substances of the world—from ants and humans and giraffes to drops of water and mighty expanses of ocean—were composed of microscopic particles invisible to the naked eye. The philosopher Democritus called these particles *atomos*, which was the Greek word for "indivisible." This term gradually evolved into the word *atom*.

During the nineteenth and early twentieth centuries, scientists conducted additional experiments that unlocked many of the secrets of the atom, including the basic atomic elements and the ways in which atoms bond together. They determined, for example, that atoms were composed of particles with negative charges (which they called electrons), positive charges (protons), and neutral charges (neutrons). Their experiments also revealed that atoms contained high volumes of energy. This was an exciting discovery to men like British physicist Ernest Rutherford, who in 1904 mused that "if it were ever possible to control at will the rate of disintegration of the [chemical] elements, an enormous amount of energy could be obtained from a small amount of matter."[1]

One year later, German physicist Albert Einstein unveiled his theory that matter can be changed into energy. He explained this insight as the mathematical formula energy (E) equals mass (m) multiplied by the speed of light squared (c^2), or $E=mc^2$. Einstein's formula accurately showed the amount of energy that could be derived from a given amount of mass—including a single atom.

Over the next several decades, scientists used Einstein's breakthrough equation to further advance their efforts to unlock the atom as an energy source. Physicists like Enrico Fermi of Italy, Otto Hahn and Fritz Strassman of Germany, and Lise Meitner of Austria all made important contributions in the 1930s.

Researchers also documented that the rare heavy metal uranium was a promising source of atomic energy. Uranium contains high levels of concentrated energy, and it exists in different forms—known as isotopes—depending on the number of neutrons in the atomic structure. Scientists also learned that the atomic structure of some of these isotopes made them good candidates for splitting, which would unleash their energy. Over time, the rare isotope uranium-235 (U-235) was identified as the best one for the atom-splitting process, which became known as fission.

A "DANGEROUS WAY TO BOIL WATER"

"What exactly is nuclear power? It is a very expensive, sophisticated, and dangerous way to boil water."—Anti-nuclear activist Helen Caldicott.

Helen Caldicott. *Nuclear Power Is Not the Answer.* New York: New Press, 2006, p. 4.

Scientists also began discussing the possibility of creating what they called a "self-sustaining chain reaction" in uranium atoms. Under this process, extra neutrons from the atom that is undergoing fission crash into and split other atoms. This in turn triggers fresh releases of energy and new waves of neutron releases that split the nuclei (centers) of other atoms. As long as this cycle was kept under control, it could become self-perpetuating and produce a steady flow of "nuclear" energy. Physicists recognized, however, that if the chain reaction proceeded *too* quickly and they lost control of the process, they could end up triggering a devastating nuclear explosion.

Entering the Nuclear Age

In 1941 Fermi and a Hungarian American colleague named Leo Szilard came up with a design for the world's first uranium chain reactor. The following year Fermi and a small group of physicists supervised the construction of the reactor on the floor of a squash court beneath an abandoned football stadium at the University of Chicago in Illinois. This primitive nuclear reactor, which became known as Chicago Pile-1, was outfitted with control rods made of cadmium, a metallic element with a strong capacity to absorb neutrons.

According to Fermi, the positioning of these rods would enable the scientists to control the speed of the chain reaction. As long as the rods were in the reactor pile containing the uranium, they would limit the number of neutrons available to split, or fission, uranium atoms. In other words, the rods would slow down the pace of chain reaction. But as the rods were slowly withdrawn, more neutrons would be freed, and the chain reaction would speed up to the point that it became self-sustaining.

The team of scientists at the University of Chicago who built the world's first uranium chain reactor in 1942. Enrico Fermi (front row, first from left) and Leo Szilard (right end of middle row) are credited with the reactor's design.

The moment of truth came on the morning of December 2, 1942, when Fermi and the other scientists assembled in Chicago tested the reactor for the first time. The rods worked flawlessly, and the nuclear reaction slowly intensified. At 3:25 P.M. Central Time, the nuclear reaction in Chicago Pile-1 reached the point at which it was self-sustaining. Fermi and his team realized that they had taken the world across the threshold of a new age of energy. One of Fermi's colleagues promptly sent a secret coded message to the U.S. government informing it of their success: "The Italian navigator has just landed in the new world."[2]

Atoms for Peace

For the next three years, most nuclear research in the United States focused on developing an atomic bomb. At that point, America was deeply engaged in World War II. This global conflict pitted Germany, Italy, and Japan—known collectively as the Axis Powers—against most of the rest of the world. In the early 1940s both sides raced to be the first to develop a nuclear bomb, fully mindful that whoever possessed such a fearsome weapon would be victorious. In the end American, British, and Canadian scientists working together on the top-secret Manhattan Project were the first to reach the finish line. They successfully detonated an atomic bomb on July 16, 1945, in a remote desert area outside Alamogordo, New Mexico. Less than a month later, two other atomic bombs developed by Manhattan Project scientists were dropped by U.S. military jets on the Japanese cities of Hiroshima (August 6) and Nagasaki (August 9). The bombs destroyed both cities and brought World War II to an end.

Once the war was over, America turned its attention back to developing nuclear technology for peaceful purposes. In 1946 Congress passed and President Harry S. Truman signed the Atomic Energy Act. This legislation created the Atomic Energy Commission, an agency specifically designed to encourage and oversee the development of nuclear science and technology. Other nations made similar investments in the postwar era, including Great Britain, Canada, and the Soviet Union.

In 1946 U.S. president Harry S. Truman signed the Atomic Energy Act into law. The law created the Atomic Energy Commission, which would oversee the development of nuclear science and technology.

Over the next several years, enthusiasm for nuclear energy continued to grow across the United States. Much of this support stemmed from America's political leaders, who painted a vision of a clean and limitless energy source capable of powering the nation's homes, schools, concert halls, fire stations, shops, and skyscrapers. In a famous December 1953 "Atoms for Peace" speech for the United Nations, President Dwight D. Eisenhower declared:

> The United States knows that peaceful power from atomic energy is no dream of the future. That capability, already proved, is here—now—today. Who can doubt, if the entire body of the world's scientists and engineers has adequate amounts of fissionable material with which to test and develop their ideas, that this capability would rapidly be transformed into universal, efficient, and economic usage. . . . Against the dark background of the atomic bomb, the United States does not wish merely to present strength, but also the desire and the hope for peace.[3]

This message was echoed by America's small but fast-growing wilderness conservation movement, which hated the hydroelectric dams that choked off the natural flow of rivers and created vast reservoirs that submerged woodlands, canyons, and other wildlife habitat. "If we learn to use [nuclear energy] properly, we won't need to harness all the rivers of the land," wrote one conservationist in a 1948 issue of the *Sierra Club Bulletin*. "At least we might wait a little while and see what happens before we drown our greatest canyons and destroy forever so much natural beauty."[4]

The Advent of Commercial Nuclear Power

The push for nuclear energy gained momentum throughout the late 1940s and 1950s. In 1949 the Atomic Energy Commission authorized the construction of a breeder reactor—a type of nuclear reactor that actually generates more material for fission than it consumes—in a remote site in central Idaho. Two years later, on December 20, 1951, this reactor became the first one in history to generate electricity from nuclear energy when it powered four 200-watt lightbulbs.

TRUMAN'S ENDORSEMENT

"In the vigorous and effective development of peaceful uses of atomic energy rests our hope that this new force may ultimately be turned into a blessing for all nations."—President Harry S. Truman.

Harry S. Truman. "Annual Message to the Congress on the State of the Union, January 6, 1947." Harry S. Truman Library and Museum. www.trumanlibrary.org/whistlestop /tap/1647.htm.

From this point forward, researchers made rapid progress in converting nuclear energy into electricity. Advances came so quickly that on August 30, 1954, Eisenhower signed the Atomic Energy Act into law. This bill, which was a major amendment to the original Atomic Energy Act of 1946, authorized private U.S. companies to build and own nuclear reactor facilities for energy production. It also expanded federal investment in nuclear research programs, provided federal funds to help companies build reactors, and promised to dispose of all nuclear waste materials generated by reactor operations.

In 1957 the United States passed the Price-Anderson Act, which shielded the young nuclear energy industry from financial liability in the event of a catastrophe at one of its facilities. That same year the first commercial electricity-generating nuclear power plant began operating in Shippingport, Pennsylvania, on December 2. The year 1957 also marked the establishment by the United Nations of the International Atomic Energy Agency. This organization was chartered to promote the peaceful use of nuclear energy and prevent the spread of nuclear weapons.

Not everyone was happy with this growing emphasis on nuclear power development. Some Americans associated it with the United States' fierce nuclear arms race with the Soviet Union, which had developed its own atomic bombs in the late 1940s. Post–World War II tensions between the Communist Soviet government and the United States became so strong, in fact, that the two nations were described as being in a state of "cold war"—a conflict in which they were constantly maneuvering to gain military, political, and diplomatic advantages over each other.

Americans who opposed the nation's nuclear arms buildup usually focused their concern on the capacity of these weapons to literally destroy the world someday. But some Americans also worried that nuclear weapons *testing* posed a growing threat to public health. By the late 1950s, in fact, critics were openly accusing the U.S. government of hiding the risks and extent of nuclear fallout from aboveground nuclear bomb tests. *Fallout* is the term used for radiation-laden dust and ash, which is blown into the atmosphere by nuclear detonations and gradually drifts back down to earth over the course of days or weeks.

Troubles for Nuclear Energy

These complaints failed to halt the growth of the nuclear power industry. On the contrary, the industry expanded rapidly for much of the 1960s and 1970s. Utility companies that earned

Technicians in Shippingport, Pennsylvania, move the reactor vessel into place during the construction of the first commercial electricity-generating nuclear power plant. The Shippingport facility started generating electricity on December 2, 1957.

revenue by supplying electricity to the public saw nuclear energy as environmentally clean and economically lucrative, especially considering all the financial help the federal government was offering. Reactor designs and capabilities evolved rapidly during this time as well. In the 1960s, wrote nuclear scientist James Mahaffey, "everything was still experimental and [reactor] designs were constantly changing as improvement came along, always moving toward higher power per unit, greater reliability, and safe containment of radiation under all conditions."[5]

A Movie Gives Nuclear Power a Black Eye

The timing of the Three Mile Island scare in Pennsylvania could hardly have been worse for the industry—or better for the makers of *The China Syndrome*, a Hollywood film centered around a potentially deadly meltdown at a fictional nuclear station in Pennsylvania. *The China Syndrome* opened in theaters across the country on March 16, 1979, just twelve days before the incident at Three Mile Island. After the Three Mile Island crisis took place, the movie—which starred Jane Fonda, Michael Douglas, and Jack Lemmon—became the most talked-about film in America. It became a box office hit and was eventually nominated for four Academy Awards.

The film painted a very bleak picture of the nuclear energy industry for American moviegoers. It depicted utility executives who cared more about profits than people's lives, and it suggested that safety procedures at America's nuclear facilities were inadequate. In reality, the incident at Three Mile Island never became as dangerous as the fictional crisis depicted in *The China Syndrome*. Nonetheless, the parallels between the film's plot and the real-life headlines from Three Mile Island made the film an effective public relations tool for anti-nuclear activists for years to come.

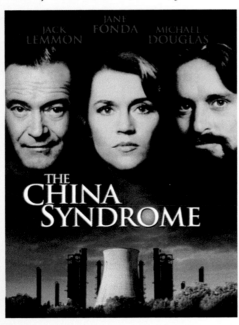

The China Syndrome, *which depicts a fictional nuclear power facility, opened in theaters just days before the real-life crisis at Three Mile Island.*

The number of fully operational commercial nuclear power plants in the United States jumped from twenty-two in 1971 to seventy-two in 1979. By the close of the 1970s—a mere two decades after the first commercial plant opened—nuclear power accounted for 12 percent of all electricity used in the United

States. The industry's momentum also was aided by a 1973 oil supply crisis in the Middle East that sent the price of gasoline soaring around the world. This jarring turn of events reminded the United States that it had become heavily dependent on foreign oil for its energy needs, and the sense among many Americans that nuclear power offered a path to energy independence was further strengthened.

In 1979, however, the nuclear power industry's image was badly tarnished by an accident at Three Mile Island, a commercial nuclear power station outside Harrisburg, Pennsylvania. On the morning of March 28, a malfunction caused a sudden loss of coolant in the core of one of the facility's two reactors, triggering a partial meltdown of its core and the release of some radioactive gases. The problem was contained before it escalated into a full-blown disaster, and no one was killed or injured. Nonetheless, some area residents were temporarily evacuated as a precaution, and news coverage of Three Mile Island inevitably pointed out that a major disaster had been narrowly avoided. Media reports included nightmarish descriptions of nuclear explosions, mass radiation poisonings, and other possible tragedies that might have occurred if the situation had spun out of control.

In late 1979 the U.S. Nuclear Regulatory Commission responded to the Three Mile Island incident by approving a set of strict new safety and inspection procedures at reactor operations. By that time, however, the damage to nuclear energy's reputation had already been done. The accident cast a black cloud over the industry that has never fully dispersed.

During the 1980s American policy makers who supported nuclear energy worked very hard to help the industry. They defended nuclear power facilities from attacks by U.S. and international environmental and public health groups that had decided that the technology posed too many dangers. Supporters also managed to pass the 1982 Nuclear Waste Policy Act, which committed the federal government to finding a permanent storage site for the disposal of high-level radioactive waste materials from nuclear power plants.

The efforts of supporters bolstered the nuclear energy industry, as did the opening or expansion of a new generation of nuclear power plants across the country. In 1983 nuclear power surpassed natural gas to become America's third-largest source of electrical power, and one year later it jumped over hydroelectric power to become the nation's second-leading source of electricity, trailing only coal. By 1989 the United States had a total of 109 nuclear power plants up and running—about one-fourth of the total plants in operation across the planet. That same year, American nuclear facilities accounted for nearly 20 percent of all the electricity used in the United States.

Disaster at Chernobyl

Despite these trends, the industry's reputation continued to decline as a direct result of another nuclear reactor accident. Unlike the Three Mile Island mishap, however, this second accident produced massive casualties and horrible levels of radiation contamination. The tragedy occurred on April 26, 1986, at Chernobyl, a nuclear power plant in Ukraine, which at that time was a part of the Soviet Union. That day, mistakes by the plant's staff triggered a massive explosion in one of the facility's four nuclear reactors. The blast immediately killed two workers and released about 50 tons (45t) of radioactive nuclear gas and dust into the atmosphere, where it drifted westward to fall across a wide swath of Soviet territory and much of Europe. Dozens of emergency workers who rushed to the site died from exposure to radiation that blanketed the grounds, and all forty thousand residents of the nearby town of Pripyat were permanently evacuated from their homes.

The final death toll from Chernobyl-related radiation exposure has been hotly debated by scientists. Some analysts believe that tens of thousands of people in the path of Chernobyl's radioactive cloud eventually died of different types of cancers and other illnesses spawned by radiation exposure, while others say that the death toll was much smaller. What is not in dispute, though, is that Soviet authorities tried to hide the accident from the rest of the world. For two days they tried to keep the explosion a secret. They only acknowledged the disaster after nuclear scientists in Sweden began reporting elevated radiation levels in their country's air, water, vegetation, and people.

When the full scale of the accident became apparent, many people concluded that governments simply could not be trusted to tell the truth about their nuclear programs. "We can understand an accident," said one citizen of Poland, which was squarely in the path of Chernobyl's radioactive fallout. "It could happen to anyone. But that the Soviets said nothing and let our children suffer exposure to this cloud for days is unforgivable."[6]

On April 26, 1986, the nuclear power plant at Chernobyl, Ukraine, suffered a massive explosion in one of the facility's nuclear reactors, spreading radiation over a wide area. The accident was an unprecedented disaster for the nuclear power industry.

Millions of people in the United States and around the world also heard chilling stories about Soviet overconfidence in their nuclear facilities. Six years before Chernobyl, for example, one Soviet expert had proclaimed that "nuclear power stations are like stars that shine all day long! We shall sow them all over the land. They are perfectly safe!"[7] When Americans learned about statements like this, they wondered whether supporters of nuclear energy in their own country knew what they were talking about.

Nuclear Power Treads Water

Since the late 1980s the nuclear energy industry has essentially treaded water—meaning that it has not made progress in meeting its goals but has also not utterly failed. Instead, the industry has spent the last two decades in a sort of limbo in the United States and much of the rest of the world. To be sure, nuclear power plants remain an important part of the energy picture in many parts of the world. The European Nuclear Society reported that as of July 2, 2012, 435 nuclear power plants were operational in thirty-one countries, with another sixty-two nuclear facilities in various stages of construction. Some of these countries remain heavily reliant on nuclear energy. France, for example, depended on nuclear energy for about 75 percent of its electricity in 2011. In the United States, meanwhile, 104 nuclear power plants were still in operation as of mid-2012. These stations provide about 20 percent of America's electricity each year. Even in traditionally nuclear-friendly places like France, though, construction of new reactors has proceeded at a much slower pace since the 1970s and early 1980s.

Pro-nuclear scientists, executives, and lawmakers who have worked to revitalize the industry suffered a severe setback on March 11, 2011. That morning, a severe earthquake off the Pacific coast of Japan created a massive, 33-foot-high tsunami (10m) that crashed into heavily populated coastal areas of the country. The combined earthquake and tsunami not only killed twenty thousand people, it also triggered terrifying reactor meltdowns and releases of radioactive material at the Fukushima Daiichi nuclear plant, located about 150 miles (241km) northeast of Tokyo. The crisis at the facility forced the evacuation of

What Went Wrong at Fukushima Daiichi

On March 11, 2011, the island nation of Japan was shaken by an 8.9 magnitude earthquake, one of the most powerful earthquakes in recorded history. The Fukushima Daiichi nuclear facility in northern Japan was unable to withstand this force, and in a matter of a few days three of its reactors suffered full nuclear core meltdowns.

The problems at Fukushima Daiichi stemmed from a loss of electrical power. First, the earthquake shut down the region's regular electrical grid. The nuclear facility then tried to use diesel-powered generators that it kept in reserve for emergencies, but a tsunami triggered by the earthquake destroyed those generators. Without power, workers at the plant had no way to operate water coolant pumps that circulate water through reactors to keep them from overheating. As a result, the water temperature and water pressure inside the reactors rose to dangerous levels. The water then began to turn to steam, which interacted with other elements in the core to create flammable hydrogen gas. Technicians at the facility tried to relieve the pressure in the cores by releasing limited amounts of radiation-tainted steam and hydrogen gas into the atmosphere, but in the end their frantic efforts failed. All three reactors underwent full meltdowns over the course of three days, and explosions from the hydrogen gas buildups caused mass discharges of radioactive materials into the atmosphere.

eighty thousand residents, whose homes may never be habitable again due to radiation contamination. It also led Japan to temporarily shut down every nuclear reactor in the country for inspection. These closures left the country without nuclear power for the first time since 1970.

The tragedy in Japan badly damaged the nuclear energy industry's image around the world. In Germany it even led to a May 2011 announcement that the government was closing eight of the country's nuclear plants immediately—and that it would shut down all seventeen of its nuclear plants by 2022. Countries like China, however, have announced their intention to keep pursuing ambitious schemes for nuclear power development.

The Fukushima Daiichi disaster also added to the industry's long-standing troubles in the United States. American utility companies have not placed an order for a new nuclear power plant since the late 1970s—despite the fact that many reactors currently in operation will have to be retired from service in the 2030s and 2040s. This decades-long absence of new construction is only partly due to environmental and public health concerns. It also is rooted in lingering frustration about cost overruns (higher-than-predicted costs) for plants that were built or expanded in America during the 1970s and 1980s. Cost overruns became so high during this era, explains the anti-nuclear Union of Concerned Scientists, that "utilities abandoned some 100 plants during construction—more than half of the planned nuclear fleet. Taxpayers and [electric utility] ratepayers reimbursed utilities for most of the more than $40 billion cost of these abandoned plants. Meanwhile, the nuclear plants that utilities did complete usually led to significant rate increases in electricity bills."[8]

Yet despite its shaky and controversial reputation, the U.S. nuclear power industry continues to survive. Numerous studies and reports about future fossil fuel shortages, environmental problems associated with oil and coal consumption, and the limitations of wind and solar power have ensured that nuclear power remains part of the global energy conversation. Indeed, millions of Americans still believe that whatever its historical shortcomings, nuclear technology continues to offer the best hope for a peaceful, prosperous, and sustainable energy future.

HARNESSING NUCLEAR ENERGY

The process of creating nuclear energy is technologically complex and enormously expensive. It rests, however, on basic scientific principles of atomic structure. Once scientists unlocked these secrets about the essential characteristics of all matter in the universe, they were able to link this information to other basic laws of nature—such as water's certain transformation into steam at high temperatures—to create the energy source now known as nuclear power.

The Basics of the Atom

Ultimately, nuclear energy is drawn from the atom. Atoms are the essential building blocks of the more than one hundred different elements that make up all matter. Some of the best-known of these elements include hydrogen, carbon, oxygen, helium, iron, copper, sodium, gold, and silver.

The core of each atom is the nucleus, which contains two types of particles called neutrons and protons. Neutrons have no electrical charge, while protons contain a positive electric charge. These positively charged protons are balanced by clouds of negatively charged electrons that circle the nucleus. The electrons are bound to the nucleus by electromagnetic force. Each element known to humankind has a unique combination of neutrons, protons, and electrons. In fact, scientists identify different versions, or isotopes, of a given element by the total number of protons and neutrons they contain. For example, the uranium-235 atom possesses 92 protons and 143 neutrons, which adds up to 235.

It is the unique atomic structure of uranium that made the element the chosen fuel for nuclear energy processes. Uranium

Atom Diagram

The atom consists of protons and neutrons in the nucleus, which are orbited by electrons.

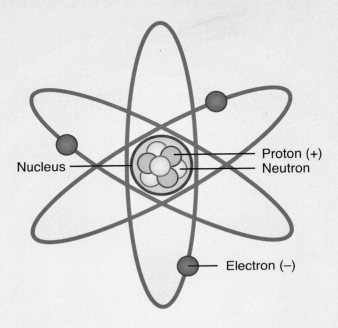

Nucleus

Proton (+)
Neutron

Electron (−)

is the heaviest of the world's natural elements. According to nuclear scientist James Mahaffey, "It was the last material created, almost as an afterthought, by the supernova destruction of a distressed star several billion years ago…. The energy locked up in uranium is millions of times more intense than the energy stored in coal or oil."[9] In addition, uranium's atomic infrastructure is not as tightly bound together as that of most other elements. In fact, it naturally decays over millennia into lesser elements. This instability makes it easier for scientists to manipulate the atomic building blocks of uranium.

Conceptually, scientists know that nuclear energy can be generated through two dramatically different treatments of uranium atoms. One process is nuclear fusion, in which nuclei from multiple atoms are merged together. Some nuclear scientists are excited about the possibilities of nuclear fusion, but it remains in the experimental phase of development. All nuclear power plants in the world currently generate their electricity through the second type of atomic alteration—nuclear fission.

The Basics of Nuclear Fission

In contrast to fusion's reliance on joining nuclei together, nuclear fission *splits* the nuclei of atoms to release their energy. When an atom is split via fission into two smaller atoms, it releases energy not only in the form of kinetic energy—energy from the motion of the fragments—but also as gamma radiation. Low levels of radiation are present in the natural world and are not harmful. Heavy exposure to gamma rays, by contrast, can cause severe burns, cancer, and genetic mutations or alterations in living organisms that are exposed to them. Gamma rays have similar properties to X-rays, though, so they can be stopped by thick walls of lead, concrete, or dirt.

Uranium atoms that undergo fission generate two or three neutrons that do not end up in the nuclei of either of the smaller atoms formed. This was an important insight for scientists, who realized that these stray neutrons had the capability to hit other

Computer artwork of a nuclear fission reaction shows a neutron (blue) about to collide with a uranium-235 nucleus (grey). The collision produces a vast amount of energy seen here as a blue and green explosion.

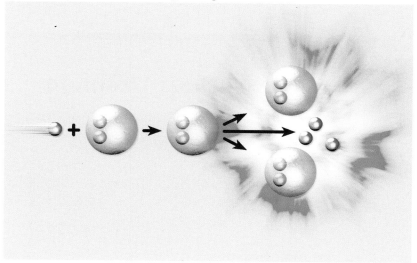

atoms so that they, too, split apart—which would in turn let loose a fresh crop of extra neutrons capable of triggering fission in yet another set of uranium atoms. The ultimate result would be a self-sustaining chain reaction of fission events that could theoretically continue without end, releasing terrific amounts of energy all the while.

Another important breakthrough for scientists was the development of techniques for enriching uranium. Under these processes, which were first developed during the 1940s and steadily improved upon in the following decades, scientists learned how to separate U-235 from U-238 so as to increase the amount of U-235 at their disposal. Mined uranium is usually composed of about 99.3 percent of the U-238 isotope and only 0.7 percent of the rare U-235 isotope. This posed a significant obstacle for nuclear physicists, since successful sustainable nuclear fission requires 3 percent or more of the uranium to be U-235. Enrichment techniques have enabled scientists to transform as much as 5 percent of natural uranium into U-235.

Turning Atoms into Electricity

All nuclear fission takes place within the vital heart of nuclear power facilities—the reactor core. It is in this section of the plant that atomic energy begins its transformation into usable electricity that makes its way into millions of living rooms, kitchens,

Learning About Uranium

Uranium is the heavy metal that serves as the raw material for the generation of nuclear energy. The element's chemical symbol is U, and it has a melting point of 2,070°F (1,132°C). Uranium was discovered in 1789 by Martin Klaproth, a German chemist. It was named after the planet Uranus, which had been discovered by astronomers eight years earlier. Scientists believe that uranium was formed by chemical reactions from a supernova that took place in outer space more than 6 billion years ago.

and office buildings around the world on a daily basis. "Imagine following a volt of electricity back through the wall socket, all the way through miles of power lines to the nuclear reactor that generated it," said science writers Marshall Brain and Robert Lamb. "You'd encounter the generator that produces the spark and the turbine that turns it. Next, you'd find the jet of steam that turns the turbine and finally the radioactive uranium bundle that heats water into steam. Welcome to the nuclear reactor core."[10] The core, in other words, is where it all begins.

A FAILED TECHNOLOGY

"Of all the failed technologies that litter the onward march of science—steam carriages, zeppelins, armoured trains—none has been so catastrophic to prosperity as the last century's attempt to generate electricity from nuclear fission."—Journalist James Buchan.

James Buchan. "A Complete Waste of Energy." *Guardian* (Manchester, UK), September 12, 2002. www.guardian.co.uk/environment/2002/sep/13/energy.comment.

The nuclear reactor core houses uranium in the form of pellets that are about 1 inch (2.5cm) long and 0.75 inches (1.9cm) wide. The pellets are stacked into long, thin metal rods, which are in turn collected together into bundles. The fission process begins when the bundled rods are submerged in water. This water acts as a coolant for the uranium, which would otherwise gradually begin to overheat.

The reaction of the uranium is also regulated by the use of control rods. These rods are made of elements that can absorb varying numbers of neutrons, depending on the extent to which they are inserted into the uranium bundle. The rods thus enable nuclear engineers to control the rate of the nuclear reaction. Control rods that are lowered into the uranium absorb greater numbers of neutrons. As the number of neutrons available for triggering chain reactions with other nuclei diminishes, so does the heat level in the core. Operators can also lower the rods completely into the uranium bundle in order to replenish the

Uranium pellets like these are stacked together to make the metal rods that are the fuel for creating nuclear power.

uranium or shut the reactor down as a safety measure. When control rods are raised out of the enriched uranium, on the other hand, the rate of fission increases, the heat level rises, and the plant can reach full capacity for electricity generation.

    Heat generated from uranium fission in nuclear reactors is used to turn water into steam. In this respect, nuclear facilities operate in much the same manner as facilities that run on coal and natural gas. For each of these types of power plants, electricity generation begins with heating vast quantities of water into steam. The steam is then pressurized and directed through pipe networks to massive networks of turbines. The turbines in nuclear power plants consist of huge rotors equipped with large blades that look a bit like airplane propellers. As the pressurized steam spins these blades around and around, the turbines produce the energy that power plant operators convert into electricity. The electricity is then dispersed via power lines to customers throughout the region.

The Reactor Containment Structure

The nuclear core area is housed inside several barriers that are designed to keep radiation from escaping into the atmosphere in either gaseous or liquid form. The first barrier is the cladding—metal tubes—that contains the nuclear fuel. The cladding is in turn surrounded by an even larger steel containment structure, sometimes known as a vessel. Finally, nuclear power plants provide their cores with a third layer of protection in the form of a huge steel or reinforced concrete shell that overlays the entire steel containment vessel. The designs of these reactor containment buildings vary, but the majority of them look like huge cylindrical cans with spherical domes.

The airtight containment shells have to meet rigorous standards of structural strength and durability. They have to be able to withstand major explosions from *within* the reactor core so as to keep radiation from leaking outside. In addition, they have to meet stringent standards for withstanding severe threats originating *outside* the building. These threats include weather events like tornadoes, tsunamis, hurricanes, earthquakes, and blizzards, as well as possible forms of terrorist attacks, such as bombs or collisions with hijacked airplanes.

Containment buildings are mandatory for all commercial power reactors and all high-power research reactors in the United States and most other countries. Some reactors, however, are not required to be outfitted in this way. Some nuclear reactors in Europe have not been equipped with containment structures, such

The open reactor at the bottom of the containment pool at the San Onofre, California, nuclear power plant glows blue from radiation.

as the ill-fated Chernobyl reactor in the former Soviet Union. Even the United States has historically carved out containment exceptions for federal research facilities with very small reactors and for government-owned reactors used in the construction of nuclear weapons and nuclear-powered submarines.

Ironically, the buildings that are most closely associated with nuclear power—cooling towers—do not serve any safety function for the plant's nuclear cores. These massive towers feature wide bases that gradually taper inward as they rise high into the heavens. Visible for miles around, cooling towers resemble fat versions of the funnels that people use to put gasoline in lawn equipment. These buildings contain machinery designed to reduce the heat of the water used in the fission process. The water treated in these facilities is either recycled for another run through the nuclear core or released from the top as harmless

Creating Plutonium in Nuclear Reactors

The explosive material in nuclear weapons is plutonium, a heavy metal that is actually created out of uranium. The nuclear fission process is dependent on uranium-235 (U-235) atoms, which account for 3 to 5 percent of the total uranium. The rest of the uranium used in nuclear plants is the isotope uranium-238, which is not a source for extracting energy. However, a U-238 atom that is struck by a stray neutron will absorb that neutron and eventually turn into an entirely different element called plutonium-239. The chemical composition of this plutonium isotope gives it enormous potential for releasing energy—which also means that it has tremendous destructive potential. Plutonium, in fact, is the explosive material used in nuclear weapons. Since most plutonium is created in nuclear reactors, it is generally considered a human-made element. Scientists, though, have found minute quantities—called trace amounts—of naturally occurring plutonium in the world.

A pellet of plutonium glows with radioactivity.

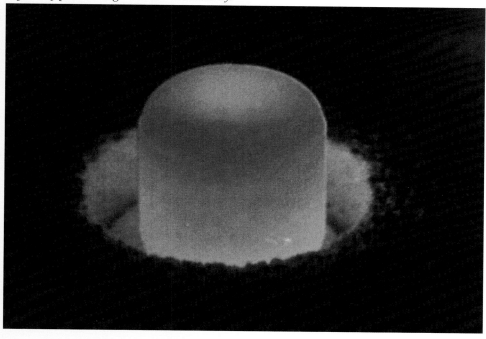

clouds of water vapor. Similar towers can also be seen at coal- and gas-powered electricity-generating plants.

The Treatment and Disposal of Nuclear Waste

The fission process in reactor operations generates a by-product called nuclear waste. Nuclear waste is depleted nuclear fuel, and it is extremely radioactive. Living creatures exposed to it face a high risk of suffering radiation sickness (also known as radiation poisoning). The immediate symptoms of radiation sickness include intense nausea, headaches, fatigue, infections, and skin blistering. In the longer term, radiation exposure is known to induce various types of life-threatening cancers in humans and animals.

A PRESIDENTIAL REASSURANCE

"All the waste in a year from a nuclear power plant can be stored under a desk."—Ronald Reagan.

Quoted in *Burlington (VT) Free Press*, February 15, 1980.

Since nuclear energy's infancy, safe disposal of radioactive waste has been one of the industry's most vexing problems. This spent fuel retains its dangerous radioactivity for many years, and each nuclear reactor generates tons of radioactive waste annually. Historically, however, waste disposal has not received the same amount of attention as reactor design and operations from scientists, engineers, lawmakers, or the public. "As a component of the nuclear power design effort," explains Mahaffey, "waste disposal . . . phase-lagged behind the more interesting bits. Any nuclear plant was able to store decades of burnt-out fuel in wet storage off to the side in the containment building, but eventually all that stuff was going to have to be put away somewhere safe. The reactor plant was not going to last forever, which was about how long the spent fuel would have to be stored."[11]

As the nuclear energy industry grew, the radioactive waste issue became a particular focus of the anti-nuclear movement in the United States. The industry's preferred solution to this issue consistently has been to establish a single underground repository for all nuclear waste. Supporters of this scheme say that placing radioactive waste deep underground in a geologically secure and stable environment is a safe and sensible solution. Some environmental activists, public health experts, and lawmakers remain deeply opposed to such an action, though, and thus far they have prevented any such facility from being established. Anti-nuclear forces say that their stance is based on genuine concern that a central repository would jeopardize the safety and welfare of people and wildlife in the region. Supporters of nuclear power charge, however, that much of the opposition is simply meant to weaken the industry. As Mahaffey writes, "If nuclear power could be prevented from moving its spent fuel from temporary storage in the reactor buildings to permanent facilities, then it would eventually choke in its own waste and die."[12]

Technicians prepare to bury a container of nuclear waste at an isolated disposal site.

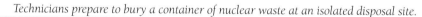

In 2002 the nuclear energy industry thought that it finally had a place to store all of its radioactive waste. That year the U.S. Congress approved the creation of a facility for the permanent storage of spent nuclear fuel and other radioactive waste at Yucca Mountain, a remote site on federal land in Nevada. In 2010, however, Democratic senator Harry Reid of Nevada and other opponents were able to kill the project by defunding it. This development forced the U.S. Department of Energy to launch a new effort to find another site for nuclear waste storage. In the meantime, nuclear power facilities have no choice but to continue storing their radioactive waste at their sites.

In Europe and other parts of the world that generate nuclear waste, serious proposals have been made to develop regional or international repositories for the disposal of high-level nuclear wastes. Studies are under way to assess how and where to establish such sites. In the meantime, according to the World Nuclear Association, an industry group, "there is a clear and unequivocal understanding that each country is ethically and legally responsible for its own wastes, therefore the default position is that all nuclear wastes will be disposed of in each of the 40 or so countries concerned."[13]

Some countries that use nuclear energy for electricity or research have also reduced their accumulations of radioactive waste through reprocessing. This is a practice in which scientists use chemicals to locate, separate, and recycle usable fuel from the waste. The United States, however, has not reprocessed nuclear waste since the 1970s because of concerns that it might contribute to nuclear weapon proliferation.

THE BENEFITS OF NUCLEAR ENERGY

As the United States and other nations around the world weigh whether to invest more money and effort in electricity-generating nuclear reactors, supporters of nuclear energy have mustered a spirited defense of the technology. Advocates of nuclear energy write books and editorials, give speeches and interviews, produce research studies, and introduce legislative bills that are designed to build public support for nuclear energy. Champions of nuclear energy emphasize the safety record of most reactor operations and trumpet all sorts of alleged advantages associated with their preferred energy source. These benefits range from nuclear technology's environmental and public health advantages over fossil fuels to the potential long-term economic benefits of nuclear energy. As journalist Michael Totty writes, though, "The argument for nuclear power can be stated pretty simply: We have no choice. If the world intends to address the threat of global warming and still satisfy its growing appetite for electricity, it needs an ambitious expansion of nuclear power."[14]

Economic Benefits

One of the major points of debate about generating electricity from nuclear power is whether this energy source makes sense financially, for either consumers or governments. Both pro- and anti-nuclear forces acknowledge that making such a determination is tricky, given all the different considerations involved. For example, the price tag for a nuclear reactor is well-defined in terms of its construction and operating costs. But calculating its total cost becomes more complicated if one also tries to take into account nuclear energy's financial benefits to the wider

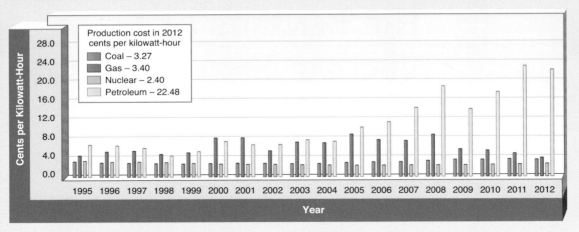

U.S. Electricity Production Costs

Overall, nuclear energy production is cheaper than fossil fuel energy production.

Production cost in 2012 cents per kilowatt-hour
- Coal – 3.27
- Gas – 3.40
- Nuclear – 2.40
- Petroleum – 22.48

Cents per Kilowatt-Hour

28.0 24.0 20.0 16.0 12.0 8.0 4.0 0.0

1995 1996 1997 1998 1999 2000 2001 2002 2003 2004 2005 2006 2007 2008 2009 2010 2011 2012

Year

Taken from: Nuclear Energy Institute/Ventyx Velocity Suite 5/13. http://www.nei.org/Knowledge-Center/Nuclear-Statistics/Costs-Fuel,-Operation,-Waste-Disposal-Life-Cycle/US-Electricity-Production-Costs.

community. These benefits include good jobs that support families. Advocates say that they also include lower health-care costs, since nuclear plants do not generate the air pollutants that are generated by coal-fired power plants. "The pro and con arguments over the cost and the economics of nuclear power are difficult to untangle," summarized the popular science website Discovery.com. "Ask 20 different experts and you will get 20 different answers."[15]

Supporters say that the economic benefits of nuclear power will become much clearer if the United States and other nations that consume lots of electricity begin building new nuclear facilities. They argue that if nuclear energy becomes more widely accepted, lending institutions will begin charging lower rates to utilities for construction loans because they will be less fearful of losing their investment. Advocates also believe that a sustained burst of reactor building would lead to lower construction costs. They assert that a greater commitment to nuclear power will result in a wider pool of manufacturers willing to make nuclear plant parts and machinery. And as the field of manufacturers becomes more crowded, they will have to keep their products reasonably priced in order to compete.

Supporters also believe that future political developments could make nuclear power more economically attractive. They note that many lawmakers in the United States and around the world are considering new regulations that would impose financial penalties or limits on emissions of carbon dioxide and other greenhouse gases responsible for climate change. If such provisions are implemented, notes Totty, "big carbon polluters like coal-produced electricity [would] look a lot more expensive compared with low-carbon sources—in particular, nuclear, wind, and hydropower."[16]

Advances in Reprocessing

The nuclear power industry also claims that new technologies now give it the capacity to address the issue of radioactive waste, which is a potential environmental and public health

Supporters say that the expansion of nuclear power usage will drive down the costs of construction of nuclear power plants and make using nuclear power even more economical.

threat and source of weapons-grade plutonium. "The idea is to reprocess that spent fuel to generate more power," writes Chuck McCutcheon in *National Geographic*. "Proponents say the know-how is available now to address the nuclear proliferation concerns that have bedeviled previous recycling plans. And they say the advanced reactors that would run on that recycled fuel would mark a new level of progress on safety."[17]

Some industry experts, scientists, and engineers believe that these new types of reactors, called Integral Fast Reactors (IFRs), might even someday end U.S. and European quests to find permanent repositories for spent nuclear fuel. IFR technology reduces the volume and radioactivity of nuclear waste by recycling uranium.

The Experimental Breeder Reactor II near Arco, Idaho, is one of the new types of reactor, called Integral Fast Reactors, that run on recycled fuel.

Charles Till, who helped develop the IFR, says that the difference between traditional nuclear power plants and IFR plants is enormous:

> The way the fuel cycle is done now is: you mine uranium; you purify the metal; you convert it to oxide; you put it in a reactor in the form of pellets; it stays in there for about three years; you take it out, and you try to find someplace to put it. The way the IFR fuel cycle would work would be: you could start with mined uranium, or you could start with fuel for present day reactors. Either one would do perfectly well. It's left in the metal form because metal is a particularly easy thing to fabricate. And so you cast it into uranium. They're put in steel jackets and loaded into the reactor. They stay in there about three to four years, and when they come out, they're put through a very simple process. One step separates out the useful materials. And then [operators can] cast the metal again back into fuel that [goes] right back into the reactor. The material that's left behind is the true, the natural waste.[18]

Till and other supporters of IFR technology also say that since plutonium and other toxic elements are recycled back into reactor operations, the remaining waste is less dangerous. Such waste would only have to be stored for hundreds of years—rather than the thousands of years required for traditional nuclear waste to degrade and become harmless. Supporters also claim that IFR reprocessing would make it much more difficult for terrorists or outlaw nations to obtain plutonium—the energy source in nuclear weapons—from nuclear power plant operations. Research into IFR and other so-called Generation IV reactor designs is ongoing, but as of 2013 there are no IFR or other Generation IV reactors in commercial operation.

Improvements in Safety

Pro-nuclear lawmakers and scientists have joined with members of the nuclear power industry in emphasizing the unblemished safety record of hundreds of nuclear energy facilities around the world. They insist that three undeniably unfortunate events—the partial meltdown of a reactor at Pennsylvania's Three Mile Island in 1979, the 1986 Chernobyl disaster in Ukraine, and the 2011 catastrophe at Japan's Fukushima Daiichi nuclear plant—have given people a misleading impression of the industry's true safety record. The U.S. industry, in particular, has expressed frustration with nuclear energy's shaky safety reputation, given that Three Mile Island took place more than three decades ago and that the international industry has experienced only three major accidents in fourteen thousand reactor-years of cumulative operation.

FUKUSHIMA MAKES NUCLEAR SKEPTIC A SUPPORTER

"As a result of the disaster at Fukushima, I am no longer nuclear-neutral. I now support the technology. A crappy old plant with inadequate safety features was hit by a monster earthquake and a vast tsunami. The electricity supply failed, knocking out the cooling system. The reactors began to explode and melt down. The disaster exposed a familiar legacy of poor design and corner-cutting. Yet, as far as we know, no one has yet received a lethal dose of radiation."—British environmentalist and author George Monbiot.

George Monbiot. "Why Fukushima Made Me Stop Worrying and Love Nuclear Power." *Guardian* (Manchester, UK), March 21, 2011. www.guardian.co.uk/commentisfree/2011/mar/21/pro-nuclear-japan-fukushima.

Advocates assert that nuclear plants in America and most other countries are safer than ever before. They have more extensive safety features and better designs than in the past. These improvements to equipment, monitoring devices, and containment shells are all designed to keep radiation from leaking into the environment under any circumstances. Nuclear plant operators also devote a great deal of time to training their personnel for every conceivable emergency situation. Workers at U.S. plants spend one out of every six weeks engaged in such training.

Members of a nuclear power plant's rapid-response team perform a safety drill. Workers at U.S. plants spend one out of every six weeks in safety training.

Nuclear expert Charles D. Ferguson points out that the Nuclear Regulatory Commission has set a safety goal of fewer than one incident of significant reactor-core damage for every ten thousand years of reactor operations. Writes Ferguson:

> One way to visualize this probability is that if 10,000 reactors were operating, it is likely that one of them would have a major accident within one year. Alternatively, for the fleet of about 100 U.S. reactors, this probability translates to a single incident of major reactor-core damage every 100 years. U.S. utilities strive to keep the probability even better, at one in 100,000 years of operation. It is estimated that the best currently operating plants have a core-damage probability of about one in 1 million years of operation.[19]

Finally, supporters of nuclear power contend it is unfair to ask the industry to always perform perfectly when other industries experience industrial accidents and damage the environment on a regular basis. "People have learned to accept that burning coal, oil, and natural gas carries risks of fires, explosions, and massive spills, and causes continuous emissions of

Nuclear Power Sparks Spirited Debate

Most prominent environmental groups based in the United States and Europe remain officially opposed to nuclear power. The leaders of these organizations have long held that nuclear energy poses too many serious threats to the environment and public health. But according to Jason Mark, editor of the environmental publication *Earth Island Journal*, "The anti-nuclear consensus among environmental policy professionals . . . does not extend to the grassroots. Rank-and-file environmentalists are divided on whether building new reactors can serve as an antidote to spiraling greenhouse gas emissions." Mark notes that on websites devoted to environmentalism and green technologies, visitors will find "a lively discussion about the merits of expanding nuclear power generation."

Jason Mark. "Will Nuclear Power Split the Green Movement?" *Earth Island Journal*, Autumn 2007. www .earthisland.org/journal/index.php/eij/article/will _nuclear_power_split_the_green_movement.

harmful fine particulates and possibly deadly gases that are altering the atmospheric chemical balance," points out pro-nuclear commentator Rod Adams. "We accept those risks because we are acutely aware of the benefits of heat and mobility."[20]

Nuclear energy advocates believe that this same standard of risk assessment should apply to nuclear power plants. Their position, according to writer Will Mara, is that "accidents involving nuclear energy, while always regrettable and potentially terrible, are a normal, albeit unfortunate, aspect of scientific progress. There has been, they say, no scientific advancement that did not come without some cost."[21]

Preservation of Wildlife Habitat

Another argument made by defenders of nuclear power production is that the technology is much friendlier to wildlife habitat and wilderness areas than all other kinds of energy production. Oil, natural gas, and coal production all depend on extracting their fossil fuel products from natural areas through drilling and mining. Both of these activities disturb fragile natural ecosystems, and coal mining in particular has been condemned by conservation groups for choking rivers and streams with shattered rock and other debris.

Environmentalists have also criticized the ecological impact of hydroelectric dams. These energy sources do not rely on fossil fuels, but they interfere with the spawning runs of salmon and other migratory fish, alter natural river-flow patterns, and submerge wildlife-rich valleys upstream of the dams under hundreds of feet of water. Nuclear energy, supporters say, does not require any such sacrifices of land or wildlife.

Pro-nuclear forces even contend that nuclear energy is environmentally superior to "green" energy sources like wind and solar power in important respects. The industry-supported Nuclear Energy Institute, for example, has pointed out that nuclear plants can generate the same amount of power as wind farms and solar photovoltaic parks on a fraction of the land necessary for wind and solar operations. Nuclear facilities also have a strong record of preserving the water quality and marine life

Many pro-nuclear organizations argue that nuclear facilities put less strain on the surrounding environment—including important wildlife habitats—than coal, gas, and hydroelectric facilities.

The Many Uses of Nuclear Technology

Nuclear technology is best known for creating electrical power and fearsome weapons, but it also plays an important role in medical research, scientific study, and industrial processes. For example, doctors use radioisotopes—radioactive elements—to diagnose and investigate the causes of disease. In many cases they are also used to treat patients. Careful exposure of patients to radiation—a practice sometimes called radiotherapy—is a particularly common treatment for certain forms of cancer. Radioisotopes are also used to test the structural integrity of machinery and buildings, and scientists have developed methods for preserving food through exposure to nuclear radiation.

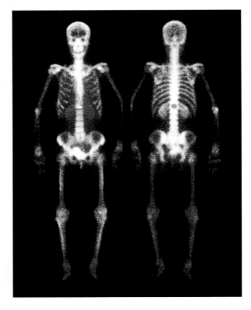

A nuclear medicine bone scan uses a radioactive substance injected into the body to reveal damage or disease.

in the nearby lakes, rivers, and coastal waters from which they draw to cool their reactors. According to the institute, operators of nuclear plants also "provide natural habitats for birds, mammals, plants, and reptiles found on or near plant sites. Many have created special nature parks or wildlife sanctuaries in order to monitor and protect endangered and threatened species."[22]

No Increased Cancer Risk

Some organizations that oppose nuclear energy have claimed that people who live in the vicinity of nuclear power plants have a greater likelihood of contracting various forms of cancer.

Nuclear power supporters have angrily denounced these charges as false or based on flawed research. They point instead to national studies such as one that was conducted in Switzerland from 2008 to 2010. This three-year study performed by the Institute of Social and Preventive Medicine at Switzerland's University of Bern (in collaboration with the Swiss Childhood Cancer Registry and the Swiss Pediatric Oncology Group) found no link between childhood cancer rates and nuclear power plant sites.

"THE GREATER EVIL"

"It really is a question about the greater evil—nuclear waste or climate change. But there is no contest anymore. Climate change is the bigger threat, and nuclear is part of the answer."—Former Greenpeace activist turned nuclear energy supporter Stephen Tindale.

Quoted in Anthony Faiola. "Nuclear Power Regains Support." *Washington Post*, November 24, 2009. http://articles.washingtonpost.com/2009-11-24/news/36857794_1_nuclear -power-nuclear-plants-nuclear-operators.

In the United States the most authoritative study on this issue was conducted by the National Cancer Institute. This study, published in a 1991 edition of the *Journal of the American Medical Association*, found no increased risk of death by cancer for Americans living near sixty-two nuclear power facilities across the country. Since that study is now more than twenty years old, however, the Nuclear Regulatory Commission announced in late 2012 that it intended to carry out a new study of cancer risks for residents near six nuclear power plants and a nuclear-fuel plant for the U.S. Navy. The facilities selected for the study are located all across the country, from California to Connecticut, and feature a mix of operational and decommissioned facilities. Members of the nuclear power industry have expressed confidence that the study, which will continue at least into 2014, will confirm that U.S. nuclear reactors do not pose a threat to the health of nearby residents.

A Weapon Against Global Warming

Members of the world's scientific community are virtually unanimous in describing global climate change, popularly known as global warming, as a massive and looming threat to life on earth. Climate experts agree that carbon dioxide and other greenhouse gases released by the burning of fossil fuels are accumulating in the atmosphere. This buildup is generating more frequent severe-weather events like hurricanes, drought-induced forest fires, and tornadoes. Greenhouse gases trapped in the upper atmosphere are also heating up the planet to the point that both polar ice caps have begun melting at a rapid rate. This development threatens to produce rising sea levels that will cover many islands and coastal areas.

COMPARING THE EMISSIONS OF COAL AND NUCLEAR

"For some reason, the smoke from a coal plant, which now is a necessary component of our electrical power consumption rate, causing cancer, global warming, and forest-destroying acid rain, is easier to forgive than fission products [nuclear waste] stored miles underground."—Nuclear scientist and author James Mahaffey.

James Mahaffey. *Atomic Awakening: A New Look at the History and Future of Nuclear Power.* New York: Pegasus, 2009, p. 308.

This grim situation has led many world leaders, scientists, environmental activists, and ordinary citizens to argue for a turn away from fossil fuels and toward renewable energy sources that do not produce greenhouse gases. Some of these people believe that nuclear power can and should play a vital role in this transition. They point out that nuclear reactors do not emit greenhouse gases and that nuclear energy currently produces far more clean energy than the other green energy industries—wind, solar, geothermal, and hydroelectric. "Even when taking into account 'full life-cycle'—including mining of uranium, shipping fuel, constructing plants, and managing waste—nuclear's carbon-dioxide discharges are comparable to the full life-cycle emissions of wind and hydropower and less than solar power,"[23] according to Totty. Most proponents of nuclear power also believe that advocates for solar and wind power understate the energy-generating limitations of those sources.

Supporters of increased investments in nuclear power also emphasize that for some time to come, energy that is not generated from nuclear reactors will probably come from coal, oil, and natural gas.

"Nuclear fission competes almost directly with fossil fuels, not with some idealized power source that carries no risk and causes no harm to the environment," stated Adams. "The electricity that Germany has refused to accept from seven large nuclear plants that the government ordered closed after Fukushima has not been replaced by the output of magically spinning offshore wind turbines or highly efficient solar panels. It

The continued use of coal-fired energy plants is increasing the levels of greenhouse gases in the atmosphere.

has been replaced by burning more gas from Russia, by burning more dirty lignite in German coal plants, and by purchasing electricity generated by nuclear-energy plants in France."[24]

For this reason, pro-nuclear organizations, lawmakers, scientists, and scholars frequently urge people to see nuclear power as a bridge that can help the world survive—and even thrive—as it makes the difficult transition from fossil fuels to wind, solar, and other renewable technologies. "Alternatively," states Ferguson, "nuclear power may experience widespread deployment in many countries over many centuries, as long as humanity remains vigilant in ensuring safe and secure use of peaceful nuclear energy."[25]

CHAPTER 4

THE DRAWBACKS OF NUCLEAR ENERGY

Nuclear energy accounts for about 20 percent of the electricity that Americans use on an annual basis. Other countries are heavily dependent on the technology as well, and the high-population nations of China and India have announced campaigns to greatly expand their nuclear energy programs. To opponents of the nuclear power industry, this state of affairs is cause for serious alarm. In their view, the advantages of nuclear power are minuscule compared to its potentially harmful impact on the environment and public health.

The Sierra Club is perhaps the largest and best-known environmental organization in the United States. When nuclear power first came on the scene in the 1940s and 1950s, the group was intrigued by the technology's potential. For most of its existence, however, the Sierra Club has rejected nuclear power. In 2012 the group confirmed its continued opposition—and offered a perspective on nuclear power that is widely shared by the industry's critics:

> The disasters at Chernobyl, Three Mile Island and Fukushima have shown [that] nuclear power can cause catastrophic damage to land, human health, and our food supply. We should pursue our cleanest, quickest, safest, and cheapest energy options first: Nuclear power comes out last in every one of those categories. In the long term, nuclear power is also unnecessary: With an intensive effort to exploit our clean energy resources, we can power our society, create good jobs, and keep our environment healthy with renewable energy such as solar and wind.[26]

Sierra Club activists protest nuclear power in New York City. The Sierra Club contends that the disasters at Three Mile Island, Chernobyl, and Fukushima have caused catastrophic damage to land, to human and animal life, and to the food supply.

Continued Concerns About Nuclear Safety

The most commonly voiced concern about nuclear reactors is that worker error, an equipment malfunction, severe weather incidents, a terrorist attack, or some other unforeseen event will breach reactor defenses and unleash a massive atomic explosion or cloud of radiation. Opponents of nuclear energy charge that the Nuclear Regulatory Commission does not adequately enforce safety standards at American nuclear facilities. They also claim that countries like Russia, China, and India that see nuclear power as an important part of their future energy mix are not making their plants as safe as possible. Critics charge that the designs, equipment, and training programs at some of these facilities are completely inadequate.

Supporters of nuclear power sometimes respond to these accusations by noting that the industry has experienced only three serious nuclear accidents—Three Mile Island, Chernobyl, and Fukushima—in more than a half century of existence. But critics charge that three accidents is three too many. In addition, they claim that the industry's history includes many near-disasters that the public does not hear much about. For example, a 2007 report prepared for the European Parliament by the anti-nuclear Greens/European Free Alliance documented multiple incidents at nuclear plants in the United States, Belgium, Hungary, France, Sweden, Germany, Taiwan, and elsewhere since the mid-1980s. According to the study's authors:

> Many nuclear safety related events occur year after year, all over the world, in all types of nuclear plants and in all reactor designs.... There are very serious events that go either entirely unnoticed by the broader public or remain significantly under-evaluated when it comes to their potential risk.... Nuclear plants are complex, hazardous facilities. It follows that this very complexity spawns a multifaceted array of potential failure mechanisms and routes, so many in fact that it is seemingly impossible to marshal these into any semblance of order.[27]

Critics of nuclear power emphasize that a serious accident at a nuclear facility could kill thousands of people and turn the surrounding area into a biological dead zone. "The magnitude of the radiation generated in a nuclear power plant is almost beyond belief," writes prominent anti-nuclear activist Helen Caldicott. "A thousand megawatt nuclear power plant contains as much long-lived radiation as that produced by the explosion of one thousand Hiroshima-sized bombs."[28] The anti-nuclear Union of Concerned Scientists, which believes that the danger posed by this kind of radiation is simply too great to accept, states, "Until long-standing problems regarding the security of nuclear plants—from accidents and acts of terrorism—are fixed, the potential of nuclear power to play a significant role in addressing global warming will be held hostage to the industry's worst performers."[29]

Uranium Mining and Native American Health

Scientists estimate that more than one-half of all uranium deposits in the United States lie under Navajo and Pueblo tribal reservation lands in the American West. For decades Native American workers have played a leading role in mining these lands, which were leased to mining companies hired by the U.S. government. In recent years, though, environmentalists, public health experts, and advocates for Native American peoples have all condemned the medical and environmental problems that these mining activities have created. Researchers have documented extremely high rates of lung cancer among Native Americans who have labored in these uranium mines. They also charge that abandoned mines and toxic debris from mining operations have poisoned the drinking water that many reservation residents use for themselves and their livestock. In 2007 Congress finally held hearings to investigate the matter. Testimony at these hearings painted a bleak picture of environmental pollution on reservation lands. As a result, in June 2008 five federal agencies with responsibilities for protecting Native American health and reservation lands agreed to clean up the contaminated uranium mining sites by 2013. At the end of 2012, the U.S. Environmental Protection Agency reported significant progress in cleaning up polluted sites. But the agency also acknowledged that it would take several more years to complete its uranium clean-up programs on reservation lands.

A uranium mine in Utah is shown here. Such mining on Native American lands has been blamed for rising rates of lung cancer among native peoples as well as an increase in contaminated drinking water.

Uncontrolled Spread of Nuclear Technology

Critics add that further expansion of nuclear power in the United States and other parts of the world increases the risk that nuclear materials from power plants might someday be obtained by terrorist groups. They assert that these groups could steal or purchase uranium or plutonium from reactor facilities (or nuclear warheads) to create their own nuclear weapons or "dirty bombs"—conventional explosives that disperse deadly radioactive material when they detonate.

Opponents have further noted that nuclear technology is spreading to countries with histories of radical politics, unpredictable behavior, and deep hostility toward the United States and other Western nations, such as Iran and North Korea. "For those nations currently vying to add nuclear capability to their arsenals, nuclear power plants offer the perfect cover," writes Caldicott. "It is only a short step from uranium enrichment for energy to the production of highly enriched uranium suitable for atomic bomb fuel, or even to reprocessed plutonium from spent fuel, suitable for bomb fuel."[30]

A TARGET FOR TERRORISTS

"Even with additional layers of security, nuclear power plants and other nuclear facilities will remain potent symbols of a country's industrial might and thus will likely continue to interest some terrorist groups in possible attacks."—Nuclear expert Charles D. Ferguson.

Charles D. Ferguson. "Psychologically Immunizing the Public Against Radiological Terrorism: Facts Can Free Their Minds." In *Social and Psychological Effects of Radiological Terrorism*, edited by Igor Khripunov, Leonid Bolshov, and Dmitriy Nikonov. Amsterdam, Netherlands: IOS, 2007, p. 17.

Concerns have also been raised about the capacity of countries like India and China, both of which are expanding their nuclear programs, to operate nuclear facilities safely. Critics worry that shortages of nuclear expertise, chronic political corruption, and shoddy government oversight of regulations for safe operation and disposal of nuclear waste will make these new reactors

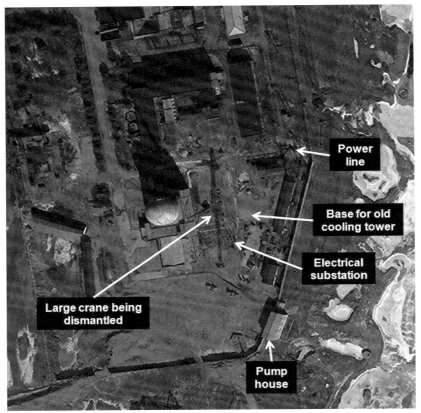

A satellite picture shows a North Korean nuclear facility suspected of processing material for nuclear weapons. Such facilities enable countries like North Korea and Iran to enrich uranium for possible use in nuclear weapons.

a menace to public health and the environment. "The Indian government has shown itself incapable of even being able to dispose of day to day garbage, let alone industrial effluent or urban sewage," said Indian political activist and writer Arundhati Roy. "How does it dare to say that it knows how to deal with nuclear waste?"[31]

The Perennial Threat of Nuclear Waste

Opponents of nuclear energy also express deep and abiding concern about the nuclear waste that reactors generate. The average one-thousand-megawatt nuclear power facility generates about 30 tons (27t) of highly radioactive waste every year, as well as even greater volumes of low- and medium-level radioactive waste. The high-level waste remains deadly for tens of thousands of years, and even the less-potent waste is toxic for hundreds of years. Worldwide, nuclear power facilities produce about 2.64 million liquid gallons or 2.27 million dry gallons (10,000 cu. m) of high-level radioactive waste on an annual basis, according to the International Atomic Energy Agency. They produce about twice that volume of low- and medium-level waste.

To date, most radioactive waste is stored in concrete-lined cooling basins or steel or concrete storage canisters at reactor sites, some of which are running out of storage room for these materials. Even advocates of nuclear power in the United States acknowledge that maintaining hundreds of different storage areas of radioactive waste across the country poses serious security, environmental, and public health challenges. In addition, the need to closely monitor these spent nuclear fuels will continue for years and even centuries after reactors are decommissioned.

In Carlton, Wisconsin, for example, many residents are openly fearful about the town's future after 2013, when a nearby nuclear power station is scheduled to shut down. The plant will leave behind 574 tons (521t) of radioactive waste, some of it in containers that were not designed for permanent storage. Federal authorities have assured the townspeople that the U.S. government will maintain a security force to watch over the waste, but many residents are not satisfied. "When they built that plant, the federal government said they were going to move the waste," said one Carlton official. "That was 35 years ago, and look where it is sitting.... They were going to bury those [nuclear fuel] rods under a mountain, and yet now they are just going to let them sit there. I have kids here and grandkids, and we're leaving them a mess."[32]

The Fruitless Search for a Federal Nuclear Waste Facility

The U.S. government has worked for decades to establish a central location for the storage of nuclear waste produced by reactors. (Radioactive waste from the production of American nuclear weapons has been stored underground at a remote location in New Mexico since 1999.) This search has taken into account the opinion of experts who agree that the safest place for nuclear waste is deep underground in stable rock formations. Thus far, however, efforts to establish such a repository have been thwarted—either by studies that have found geographic flaws in potential sites or by opposition from residents and lawmakers of states that have been identified as potential hosts.

For a while it appeared that a national nuclear waste storage facility was going to be established at Yucca Mountain, a remote ridge located on federal land in south-central Nevada, about 100 miles (160km) from Las Vegas. In 2002 the U.S. Congress for-

The federal government's nuclear waste storage facility at Yucca Mountain, Nevada, was approved in 2002, but continued protests by environmentalists led to the defunding of the project in 2009.

mally approved construction of a federal waste storage facility at the location. Continued protests by environmental groups and Nevada residents kept the issue alive, however, especially since the facility would take decades to build. In 2009 opponents of the project rejoiced when the newly installed administration of President Barack Obama announced that it did not see Yucca Mountain as a viable option for storage of the country's nuclear waste. One year later, funding for development of the Yucca Mountain waste site was formally terminated by legislation championed by Nevada senator and U.S. Senate majority leader Harry Reid.

RENEWABLES ARE THE FUTURE

"I would argue that it's entirely possible to close the nuclear plants, close the vast majority of fossil fuel plants, and use renewables and energy efficiency to meet our energy needs to reduce carbon emissions by 80 percent by 2050, and nobody's lifestyle has to change."—Michael Mariotte of the Nuclear Information and Research Service.

Quoted in Jason Mark. "Will Nuclear Power Split the Green Movement?" *Earth Island Journal*, Autumn 2007. www.earthisland.org/journal/index.php/eij/article/will_nuclear _power_split_the_green_movement.

In 2012 a special commission appointed by Obama to seek alternatives to Yucca Mountain urged the United States to find a geologically viable site that also had local support. The commission noted that jobs and other economic benefits have helped several European nations gain local support for their own proposed nuclear waste depots. The commission also warned that finding a solution to this problem could not wait for another decade or two. "This generation has a fundamental, ethical obligation to avoid burdening future generations with the entire task of finding a safe, permanent solution for managing hazardous nuclear materials they had no part in creating,"[33] wrote the commission.

Meanwhile, the decades of uncertainty over storage of radioactive waste has further hardened opposition to nuclear energy in general. Most critics do not see the establishment of a permanent central site as a good solution, anyway. They point out that even if such a depot opened, radioactive waste generated all across the country would still have to be transported there via rail, truck, or ship. None of these transport options are immune from accidents or terrorist attacks that could trigger widespread contamination and death.

Foes of nuclear power also do not have much faith in Integral Fast Reactors (IFRs) or other experimental technologies that would reduce the volume and radioactivity of waste by processing spent nuclear fuel back into reactor operations. Their skepticism has intensified with the release of studies such as a 2010 report from the International Panel on Fissile Materials, an organization of nuclear arms experts. The panel raised pessimistic questions about the safety, reliability, security, and economic wisdom of building these types of reactors. "So far, the new designs are mostly paper studies, and the prospect of a strong effort to develop the burner reactors is at best uncertain," the panel wrote. "The economic and nonproliferation arguments against such reactors burn strong."[34]

The Threat of Radiation Leaks

The nuclear energy industry has been accused by some opponents of spreading disease in communities that host nuclear power stations. Critics charge that the cumulative impact of small but daily releases of radiation from reactor facilities—either from accidents or as part of normal operations—trigger higher rates of cancer in the surrounding community. Some health studies have seemed to confirm this belief. The Radiation and Public Health Project, for example, has published several reports linking nuclear radiation to high childhood cancer rates. Other health studies, however, have not found higher levels of cancer or other diseases near reactor sites. Many critics of nuclear power have urged further research into this issue by independent scientists who are unaffiliated with the nuclear industry or with federal agencies like the Nuclear Regulatory Commission, which has historically been supportive of the industry. "Congress should appropriate funds supporting a truly independent

David Lochbaum, director of the Nuclear Power Project for the Union of Concerned Scientists, testifies before Congress after the nuclear accident in Fukushima, Japan, in 2011.

study on cancer rates near U.S. reactors," said Samuel S. Epstein, chair of the Cancer Prevention Coalition. "The American public deserves to know just what these machines have done to them, so that future energy policies will better protect public health."[35]

Environmental groups have also leveled complaints about contamination of local water supplies by radiation leaks from nuclear facilities. According to the Union of Concerned Scientists:

> There have been more than 400 accidental leaks, some involving millions of gallons of contaminated water. Some of the leaks remained undetected for years. Nearly every nuclear plant in the country has experienced at least one accidental leak. The Nuclear Regulatory Commission has breached its contract with the public by repeatedly tolerating unmonitored and uncontrolled leaks of radioactively contaminated water into the ground and nearby waterways.[36]

Historically, however, opponents of nuclear energy have not made "everyday" radiation emissions a major focus of their antinuclear campaigns. They have instead emphasized the risks of major nuclear accidents, the nuclear waste storage problem, and their preference for other technologies for fighting global warming.

An Unwise Economic Investment

Another frequent charge leveled against nuclear power by opponents is that nuclear energy facilities simply do not make much economic sense. Critics note that construction and operation

Environmental groups and some energy experts want to see less money given to nuclear power and more given to the development of energy sources like wind and solar, as seen here.

A Truly Limitless Energy Source?

Many advocates of nuclear power tout the technology's long-term promise, since it does not rely on fossil fuel deposits that will eventually be exhausted. Foes of nuclear energy point out, though, that technologies for nuclear fission do currently rely on uranium, an element that has only been found in extremely limited quantities. Some studies indicate that the world has enough uranium to power nuclear reactors for another two hundred years or so, but scientists have noted that this time estimate could drop dramatically if the world were to invest heavily in new nuclear facilities.

costs for nuclear reactor stations and storage of nuclear waste have frequently exceeded forecasts—sometimes by billions of dollars per facility. Environmental organizations and other opponents also note that the entire U.S. nuclear industry has historically depended for its very existence on massive packages of taxpayer money from the federal government. They say that these packages of financial aid, known as subsidies, should be brought to an end. "Historical subsidies to nuclear power have already resulted in hundreds of billions of dollars in costs paid by taxpayers and [electric utility] ratepayers," stated a 2010 report from the Union of Concerned Scientists. "With escalating plant costs and more competitive power markets, the cost of repeating these failed policies will likely be even higher this time around."[37]

Environmental groups and some energy experts would like to see the United States and other countries divert the dollars currently going to nuclear power to those other "power markets"—renewable energy sources like wind and solar power. They emphasize that every penny that goes to support nuclear technology is a penny that is not available for wind, solar, or geothermal research.

Many of these same critics believe that renewables have already proved themselves to be a better bet than nuclear energy. "The costs of renewable energy such as wind and solar power are cheaper, and getting cheaper all the time," explains journalist Michael Totty. "By contrast, nuclear is more expensive, and getting more expensive all the time."[38]

Not the Answer to Global Warming

Bill McKibben is a prominent environmental writer who founded the 350.org anti–global warming group. He has been one of the most vocal advocates of switching government support from nuclear energy to wind and solar energy technologies that can combat climate change. According to McKibben:

> The worst thing you can say about [nuclear energy], at least aside from nuclear waste and plutonium and terrorism, the worst thing you can say about it is it wastes an incredible amount of money. It will only happen with massive, massive government subsidy. And if we're going to subsidize something, there are a lot of technologies that offer a lot more kilowatt hours for the buck than trying to build giant nuclear power stations.[39]

Climate scientists, lawmakers, and environmental organizations that are campaigning for new energy strategies that will reduce the impact and severity of global warming have been critical of nuclear power on other grounds as well. Environmental journalist Mark Hertsgaard points out that nuclear energy "produces only electricity, but electricity amounts to only one-third of America's total energy use (and less of the world's). Nuclear power thus addresses only a small fraction of the global warming problem, and has no effect whatsoever on two of the largest sources of carbon emissions: driving vehicles and heating buildings."[40]

Finally, critics point out that nuclear power plants currently take a decade or more to build and make operational so that they can begin generating electricity. But global climate change is already occurring, and the world needs green energy alternatives that will not take so long to get up and running. Many energy experts and environmental activists believe that renewable energy sources like wind and solar can be implemented much more quickly, especially if those industries receive more finan-

One of the most vocal advocates of switching government support from nuclear energy to wind and solar power is Bill McKibben (in blue). He founded 350.org to fight global warming and promote wind and solar power.

cial support from the U.S. government. "The danger of wasting money and time in the fight against global warming is the nightmare that haunts me the most," said McKibben, "because this wave is breaking over our heads, and we'd better choose right the first time."[41]

NUCLEAR ENERGY IN THE TWENTY-FIRST CENTURY

Some energy experts believe that nuclear energy is poised for new growth and that it has the capacity to meet a much higher percentage of our total energy needs in the decades to come. This confidence is based in large part on innovative ideas and technologies for nuclear power generation. It also stems from growing evidence that greenhouse gases from traditional fossil fuel energy sources are unnaturally warming the planet. Other observers, though, think that nuclear energy is unlikely ever to become a centerpiece of the global energy picture—and that it might even vanish from the scene over the next century.

Nuclear Power After Fukushima

The March 2011 disaster at the Fukushima Daiichi nuclear plant in Japan had a major impact on nuclear power programs in many parts of the world. Critics of nuclear energy research portrayed the tsunami-sparked crisis as yet another sign (like Three Mile Island and Chernobyl) that the technology simply is not safe enough for humankind to use in meeting its energy needs. In the United States the incident intensified calls for the government to increase its investments in non-nuclear research and more closely oversee the nuclear industry's operations. In Belgium, Germany, Italy, and Switzerland, governments announced their intention to shut down nuclear power plants or dramatically reduce their reliance on nuclear energy. In places like Germany, these promises were issued after citizens carried out massive anti-nuclear protests in some of its biggest cities.

Other countries, however, expressed determination to move forward with nuclear research and nuclear power plant con-

struction. These nations included China and India, the two most
heavily populated countries in the world. India, for example, is
pushing forward with such a massive expansion of its nuclear
program that it expects to get 25 percent of its electricity from
nuclear reactors by 2050—up from 4 percent in 2012.

Another steadfast defender of nuclear energy after Fukushima was France, which has long depended on the technology
for 75 to 80 percent of its energy. But even in France, anxiety
about the safety of nuclear power rose after Fukushima—and
after environmental activists with Greenpeace France broke into
two reactor facilities in December 2011 just to show that it could
be done. In 2012 newly elected French president François Hol-
lande openly spoke about the need to reduce his nation's dependence on nuclear energy. "I think there is a lot of change in the

*A nuclear power plant under construction in India. India has expanded its
nuclear program and expects to get 25 percent of its electricity from nuclear
reactors by 2050.*

opinion," said Greenpeace France spokesperson Yannick Rousselet. "They [the French people] are not in favor of stopping [using nuclear power] today. But clearly, I think now a big majority of people think that we must phase out."[42]

Racing to Find the Energy Source of the Twenty-First Century

Every significant potential source of energy is currently being investigated by scientists and researchers around the world. Oil, gas, and coal companies are exploring sophisticated new technologies for extracting and refining previously inaccessible or unusable fossil fuel deposits. Advocates for wind, solar, geothermal, and other renewable technologies are pressing governments and corporations alike to devote more money and resources to those green alternatives. Supporters of nuclear power are engaged in this race as well, oftentimes with major financial assistance from national governments.

Microsoft cofounder Bill Gates speaks to the media in China about discussions to jointly develop a new kind of nuclear reactor. Gates wants governments to not only develop nuclear energy but other green energies as well.

In some cases the perpetual quest for new and better forms of energy is being driven by the desire for corporate profit, economic expansion, and increased energy independence. In other instances the urgency behind research comes from the threat of global climate change and other environmental concerns. In the case of nuclear energy research, most observers would agree that the drive to build better nuclear reactors is being propelled by a combination of economic and environmental considerations.

MAKING NUCLEAR POWER PRACTICAL

"I would like nuclear fusion to become a practical power source. It would provide an inexhaustible supply of energy, without pollution or global warming."—Physicist Stephen Hawking.

Stephen Hawking. "10 Questions for Stephen Hawking." *Time*, November 15, 2010. www.time.com/time/magazine/article/0,9171,2029483,00.html.

Many of the nuclear scientists and energy experts who are charting new paths in nuclear power research are confident that they can open the door to a bright new energy future. They have been joined in this effort by wealthy investors like Bill Gates, cofounder of the Microsoft computer company. Says Gates:

To have the kind of reliable energy we expect, and to have it be cheaper and zero carbon, we need to pursue every available path to achieve a really big breakthrough. I certainly don't want the government to only pick a few paths, because our probability of success is much higher if we're pursuing many, many paths. Think about all the people who are getting up every day and working on solutions that may seem kind of delusional even though the odds against them are higher than they realize. The world needs all these people trying things out and believing in them. In IT [information technology, the development of computers and telecommunications], there were tons of dead ends—but there was enough of a success rate to have an unbelievable impact.[43]

New Frontiers in Reactor Design

Historically, the global nuclear energy industry has classified its fleet of reactors by their age. Generation I reactors were built during the 1950s and 1960s. Most of them are no longer in operation, since they have been replaced by newer designs. Generation II reactors collectively refer to a variety of reactor designs that came on the scene in the 1970s and were built up until the close of the 1990s. These reactors account for the vast majority of nuclear reactors currently in operation around the world.

Generation II+ and Generation III reactors are modified versions of Generation II reactors. These are regarded by industry scientists and engineers as significant improvements over older reactor designs, but research into so-called Generation IV reactors is what has them most excited. According to nuclear expert Charles D. Ferguson, Generation IV reactors feature "truly revolutionary designs . . . [that] could offer significant breakthroughs, especially in safety and efficiency."[44] Nuclear experts believe that one or more of these new reactor designs could be commercially introduced by the mid-twenty-first century.

Many Generation IV designs are based on the Integral Fast Reactor blueprint, which seeks to recycle and consume virtually all spent uranium and plutonium that comes out as waste material in existing nuclear reactors. "Integral Fast Reactors can be the game-changing technology that can lead us out of many of the crises humanity faces," declares the Science Council for Global Initiatives, a pro-nuclear organization of nuclear scientists and climatologists. "It is so far beyond the current generation of nuclear power systems that to compare one with the other would be like comparing a Model T to a Lexus."[45]

There are six basic reactor design models under the Generation IV banner—three thermal reactors and three fast reactors. The three thermal reactor designs are the very-high-temperature reactor, which uses graphite for controlling fission rates and helium gas as a coolant; the supercritical-water-cooled reactor, which uses the traditional coolant of water but at much higher temperatures and pressure than current reactor models; and the molten-salt reactor. The three Generation IV fast reactor designs currently undergoing research and development are the gas-cooled fast reactor, the lead-cooled fast reactor, and the sodium-cooled fast reactor.

The nuclear research and development community is uncertain at this point which—if any—of these options will ultimately win out. But the Energy Department, which provides funding for much of the Generation IV research, has expressed high expectations for the program. "The goal of the Gen IV Nuclear Energy Systems is to address the fundamental research and development (R&D) issues necessary to establish the viability of next-generation nuclear energy system concepts to meet tomorrow's needs for clean and reliable electricity, and non-traditional applications of nuclear energy," stated the department's Office of Nuclear Energy. "Successfully addressing the fundamental R&D

The Rajasthan nuclear power plant in India is one of the new generation of nuclear facilities. The United Nations has said India's reactors are the safest in the world.

issues will allow Gen IV concepts that excel in safety, sustainability, cost-effectiveness, and proliferation risk reduction to be considered for future commercial development and deployment by the private sector."[46]

Energy Options Compete for Supporters

Other experimental reactor designs are attracting investor dollars as well. For example, Gates has invested millions of dollars in TerraPower, a company that is developing a so-called traveling wave reactor that runs on depleted uranium. He explains:

> Ninety-seven percent of uranium we don't use (in traditional reactors), and we use that 97 percent. So our fuel is free. In fact, we can even use waste from normal reactors and burn it up. . . . So this is a design that on paper is phenomenal. But the challenge to actually get it built, prove the economics—doing it is a high-risk activity, and so we're talking to all sorts of people all over the world about partnering to actually build one of these things.[47]

Opponents of nuclear energy, though, are skeptical of the industry's ability to meet these goals. Some people believe that the nature of nuclear energy means that it will always be a health and environmental risk in the event of terrorist attacks or severe weather events. Others assert that the planet simply does not have time for these experimental reactors to be finalized and tested. Anti-nuclear activist Helen Caldicott writes:

> Designs are so complex that they will be nowhere near completion until 2030 at the earliest with 2045 a more practical date. Obviously they have not been conceived to make any difference to the global warming problem now. The situation is urgent and must be addressed at once. The money allocated to these new reactors could be used right now to mass produce renewable energy technologies that are currently available, and only these renewable technologies will have a positive effect to reduce global warming gases.[48]

Megatons to Megawatts

Since the late 1980s the United States has signed a series of nuclear bomb reduction treaties with Russia and other countries of the former Soviet Union. These so-called disarmament treaties have dramatically reduced the size of the nuclear arsenals in all of these countries. In addition, they have given U.S. nuclear power plants a significant new source of fuel for electricity production.

The nuclear arms control agreements between the United States and Russia have also supported the creation and maintenance of a Megatons to Megawatts program. Under this program, America purchases uranium from decommissioned Russian nuclear warheads for use in U.S. power plants. In many years this source has accounted for nearly half of the nuclear fuel used in America for electricity generation. By comparison, only about 5 percent of American nuclear power comes from decommissioned American warheads. According to the World Nuclear Association, the Megatons to Megawatts program had delivered about 450 tons (408t) of highly enriched uranium to the United States as of July 2012—the equivalent of about eighteen thousand nuclear warheads.

Russian officials announce the Megatons to Megawatts program in 2002, allowing the conversion of Russian nuclear weapons into fuel for nuclear power plants.

This line of thought has gained wind and solar companies some wealthy investors of their own. The Internet giant Google, for instance, invested more than $1 billion in wind and solar energy projects across the United States from 2010 through early 2013. Under President Barack Obama, the U.S. government has also boosted its financial support for green energy research.

LEAVING THE COLD WAR BEHIND

"Nuclear power was a Cold War creation. It represented massive concentration of power and reflected the geopolitics of a post–World War II era. Today, however, new technologies are giving people the tools they need to become active participants in an interconnected world. . . . We should pursue an aggressive effort to bring the full range of decentralized renewable technologies online: solar, wind, geothermal, hydro and biomass. . . . Our common energy future lies with the sun, not with uranium."— Economist and environmentalist Jeremy Rifkin.

Jeremy Rifkin. "No Nukes!" *Los Angeles Times*, September 29, 2006. http://articles.la times.com/2006/sep/29/opinion/oe-rifkin29.

New Fuels and Technologies

Scientists are also exploring the possibility of using thorium instead of uranium as nuclear fuel, both in existing and experimental reactor designs. Thorium is a silvery white metal discovered by Swedish chemist Jöns Jakob Berzelius early in the nineteenth century. Berzelius named the element after Thor, the Norse god of thunder. Unlike uranium-235 (U-235), the isotope that powers current nuclear reactors, thorium is not a fissile material. That means that it cannot be used in its natural form as fuel for a self-sustaining nuclear reaction. But thorium is fertile nuclear material, which means that if it is placed in a nuclear reactor, it can produce an element—uranium-233 (U-233)—which can be used for nuclear fission.

Thorium has several significant advantages over uranium. It is three to four times more abundant than uranium in the natural world, and it generates energy more efficiently than U-235. Thorium also generates much less radioactive waste than uranium because thorium atoms break down into fewer unusable atoms than do uranium atoms. This also means that thorium-based reactors generate much less plutonium-239, the radioactive isotope used to produce nuclear bombs. Thorium-based reactors do produce another possible weapons material, the isotope uranium-233, but this element is extremely difficult to separate into a form that can be used for weapons production. These considerations appeal to people who worry about terrorist groups or unstable governments gaining access to nuclear weapons materials.

Thorium, first discovered by Jöns Jakob Berzelius in the early nineteenth century, is being explored by scientists to see whether it could be a viable alternative to uranium in the production of nuclear power.

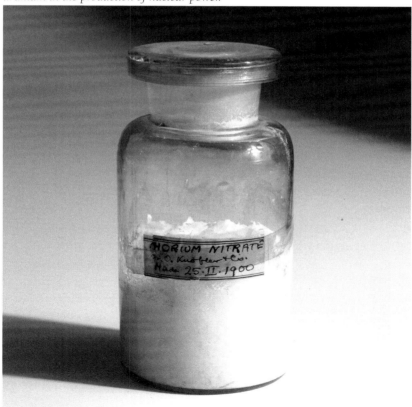

Thorium-fueled reactors have even been promoted as a way to reduce the world's existing stockpiles of plutonium. Scientists believe that plutonium can be used as a seed fuel for thorium reactors. "A seed is necessary because it's harder to start a nuclear chain reaction with thorium than with uranium,"[49] explains the science and technology magazine *Wired*. Finally, advocates say that thorium-based reactors are designed so that they will not melt down or blow up, thus sparing the world future catastrophic events like Chernobyl and Fukushima.

Other observers believe, however, that thorium-powered reactors are not the magic energy solution that some supporters make them out to be. Critics say that outfitting existing reactors to run on thorium—or making new thorium-fueled reactors—would be incredibly expensive. They also insist that thorium supporters are exaggerating its other benefits. This skeptical stance is held not only by anti-nuclear environmental organizations and public health advocates, but also by some scientific agencies. In September 2012, for example, Britain's Department of Energy and Climate Change released a study declaring that thorium's "theoretical advantages regarding sustainability, reducing radiotoxicity, and reducing [nuclear] proliferation risk . . . are often overstated."[50]

Scientists have also been studying the possibility of capturing energy through nuclear fusion—the joining of two atoms—rather than nuclear fission, the atom-splitting process on which nuclear power plants have always relied. Thus far, however, researchers have been unable to solve this puzzle and unlock fusion's potential for energy creation. "An oft-told joke in energy research is that nuclear fusion is the energy source of the future and always will be," wrote Ferguson. "Scientists and engineers have produced uncontrolled fusion reactions with nuclear weapons, [but] they have struggled to harness this power source in a controlled manner. The main difficulty is in maintaining the required intense temperatures and pressures."[51]

A Hazy Future

Given all the different and complex environmental, political, economic, and scientific forces that are influencing the world

Decommissioning Nuclear Power Plants

Nuclear power facilities do not last forever. The first nuclear power plants were designed to operate for thirty to forty years, while newer reactors typically are built to last fifty to sixty years. When a nuclear power plant is identified for permanent closure and loses its license to operate, the electric company that owns the facility has to take a wide range of steps to remove it from service. This process is called decommissioning.

In the United States the Nuclear Regulatory Commission oversees the decommissioning of all nuclear power plants. Nuclear Regulatory Commission rules are designed to protect both the public and the workers during every phase of the decommissioning process. The regulations are particularly strict and detailed for the two most sensitive aspects of decommissioning—cleanup of radioactively contaminated areas of the plant and removal of leftover radioactive fuel.

The cooling tower of an old nuclear power plant is imploded as part of the plant's decommissioning.

of nuclear energy, it is impossible to know just what role nuclear power will play in the world as it moves deeper into the twenty-first century. Perhaps a nuclear disaster of truly horrible dimensions will turn the planet against the technology for good. Maybe an innovation in wind or solar power or some other renewable energy resource will make nuclear power obsolete. Or perhaps the pivotal discovery that takes the world down a new and more sustainable energy path will come from nuclear scientists who unlock the secret of nuclear fusion or produce a radioactive waste–free reactor.

Whatever its ultimate fate, it seems almost certain that nuclear power will remain a big part of conversations about finding a permanent solution for the world's energy needs. This is especially true given the rising urgency of addressing global warming. Some scientists, lawmakers, and environmentalists are convinced that nuclear technology gives the world the best—and maybe the only—chance to maintain its current living standards without ruining the planet. Others in those same communities, however, remain equally convinced that more fully embracing nuclear power will have tragic results.

Chapter 1: The History of Nuclear Energy

1. Quoted in U.S. Department of Energy. *The History of Nuclear Energy*. Washington, DC: U.S. Department of Energy, 2006. http://energy.gov/sites/prod/files/The%20History%20 of%20Nuclear%20Energy_0.pdf.

2. Quoted in Cynthia Kelly, ed. *The Manhattan Project: The Birth of the Atomic Bomb in the Words of Its Creators, Eyewitnesses, and Historians.* New York: Black Dog and Leventhal, 2007, p. 86.

3. Dwight D. Eisenhower. "Address Before the General Assembly of the United Nations, December 8, 1953." *Congressional Record*, January 7, 1954. www.presidency.ucsb.edu/ws /index.php?pid=9774.

4. Quoted in Kevin Hillstrom. *U.S. Environmental Policy and Politics: A Documentary History.* Washington, DC: CQ, 2010, p. 345.

5. James Mahaffey. *Atomic Awakening: A New Look at the History and Future of Nuclear Power.* New York: Pegasus, 2009, p. 303.

6. Quoted in John Greenwald and Ken Olsen. "Disaster Judgment at Chernobyl." *Time*, July 20, 1987, pp. 44–45.

7. Quoted in Richard Rhodes. *Nuclear Renewal: Common Sense About Energy.* New York: Whittle/Viking, 1993, p. 91.

8. Union of Concerned Scientists. *Nuclear Power: A Resurgence We Can't Afford.* Washington, DC: Union of Concerned Scientists, August 2009. www.ucsusa.org/assets/documents /nuclear_power/nuclear-economics-fact-sheet.pdf.

Chapter 2: Harnessing Nuclear Energy

9. Mahaffey. *Atomic Awakening*, pp. 4–6.

10. Marshall Brain and Robert Lamb. "How Nuclear Power Works." HowStuffWorks. www.howstuffworks.com/nuclear-power.htm.

11. Mahaffey, *Atomic Awakening*, pp. 304–305.

12. Mahaffey, *Atomic Awakening*, p. 305.

13. World Nuclear Association. "International Nuclear Waste Disposal Concepts," April 2012. www.world-nuclear.org/info/inf21.html.

Chapter 3: The Benefits of Nuclear Energy

14. Michael Totty. "The Case for and Against Nuclear Power." *Wall Street Journal*, June 30, 2008. http://online.wsj.com/article/SB121432182593500119.html.

15. Joanna Burgess. "10 Pros and Cons of Nuclear Power." Discovery.com, 2010. http://dsc.discovery.com/tv-shows/curiosity/topics/10-pros-cons-nuclear-power.htm.

16. Totty. "The Case for and Against Nuclear Power."

17. Chuck McCutcheon. "Can Nuclear Waste Spark an Energy Solution?" *National Geographic*, September 1, 2010. http://news.nationalgeographic.com/news/2010/08/100831-can-nuclear-waste-spark-an-energy-solution.

18. Quoted in *Frontline*. "Nuclear Reaction: Why Do Americans Fear Nuclear Power?" PBS, April 1997. www.pbs.org/wgbh/pages/frontline/shows/reaction/interviews/till.html.

19. Charles D. Ferguson. *Nuclear Energy: What Everyone Needs to Know*. New York: Oxford University Press, 2011, p. 143.

20. Rod Adams. "Nuclear Power After Fukushima: It Is, Still, the Energy of the Future." *National Review*, June 20, 2011, p. 41.

21. Will Mara. *The Chernobyl Disaster: Legacy and Impact on the Future of Nuclear Energy*. New York: Marshall Cavendish, 2011, p. 84.

22. Nuclear Energy Institute. "Key Issues: Protecting the Environment—Ecology." www.nei.org/Key-Issues/protectingtheenvironment/ecology.

23. Totty. "The Case for and Against Nuclear Power."

24. Adams. "Nuclear Power After Fukushima," p. 41.

25. Ferguson. *Nuclear Energy*, p. 207.

Chapter 4: The Drawbacks of Nuclear Energy

26. Sierra Club. "Why Nuclear Power Doesn't Make Sense." www.sierraclub.org/nuclear/factsheet.aspx.

27. Georgui Kastchiev et al. *Residual Risk: An Account of Events in Nuclear Power Plants Since the Chernobyl Accident in 1986.* Greens/European Free Alliance, May 2007. http://archive .greens-efa.eu/cms/topics/dokbin/181/181995.residual _risk@en.pdf.

28. Helen Caldicott. *Nuclear Power Is Not the Answer.* New York: New Press, 2006, p. 14.

29. Union of Concerned Scientists. "UCS Position on Nuclear Power and Global Warming," March 5, 2007. www.ucsusa .org/nuclear_power/nuclear_power_and_global_warming /ucs-position-on-nuclear-power.html.

30. Caldicott. *Nuclear Power Is Not the Answer*, p. 141.

31. Quoted in Wieland Wagner. "India Pursues Massive Nuclear Expansion." *Der Spiegel*, November 23, 2012. www.spiegel .de/international/world/india-pushes-forward-with-massive -expansion-of-nuclear-capabilities-a-868662.html.

32. Quoted in Ron Seely. "Questions Arise About Shuttering of Kewaunee Nuclear Power Reactor." *Wisconsin State Journal*, November 3, 2012. http://host.madison.com/news/local /environment/questions-arise-about-shuttering-of -kewaunee-nuclear-power-reactor/article_8ab13fd6 -25ea-11e2-b3f4-001a4bcf887a.html.

33. Quoted in Matthew L. Wald. "Revamped Search Urged for a Nuclear Waste Site." *New York Times*, January 26, 2012. www.nytimes.com/2012/01/27/science/earth/nuclear-waste -panel-urges-consent-based-approach.html.

34. Thomas B. Cochran et al. *Fast Breeder Reactor Programs: History and Status.* International Panel on Fissile Materials, February 2010. http://fissilematerials.org/library/rr08.pdf.

35. Samuel S. Epstein. "Nuclear Power Causes Cancer: What Industry Doesn't Want You to Know." *Huffington Post*, August 4, 2009. www.huffingtonpost.com/samuel-s-epstein /nuclear-power-causes-canc_b_251057.html.

36. Union of Concerned Scientists. "Regulatory Roulette: The NRC's Inconsistent Oversight of Radioactive Releases from Nuclear Power Plants," September 28, 2010. www.ucsusa .org/nuclear_power/nuclear_power_risk/safety/regulatory -roulette-the.html.

37. Doug Koplow. *Nuclear Power: Still Not Viable Without Subsidies*. Cambridge, MA: Union of Concerned Scientists, February 2011. www.ucsusa.org/assets/documents/nuclear _power/nuclear_subsidies_report.pdf.

38. Totty. "The Case for and Against Nuclear Power."

39. Quoted in Amy Goodman and Juan González. "Environmentalist, 350.org Founder Bill McKibben on *Eaarth: Making a Life on a Tough New Planet*." Democracy NOW!, April 15, 2010. www.democracynow.org/2010/4/15/mckibben.

40. Mark Hertsgaard. "Nuclear Energy Can't Solve Global Warming." *San Francisco Chronicle*, August 7, 2005. www .sfgate.com/green/article/Nuclear-energy-can-t-solve-global -warming-Other-2649418.php#page-1.

41. Bill McKibben. "Atomic Idyll." OnEarth, September 1, 2007. www.onearth.org/article/atomic-idyll.

Chapter 5: Nuclear Energy in the Twenty-First Century

42. Quoted in Voice of America. "Year After Fukushima, Nuclear Energy Divides Europe," March 8, 2012. www.voanews .com/content/a-year-after-fukushima-nuclear-energy -divides-europe-142100153/180606.html.

43. Quoted in Jeff Goodell. "Q&A: Bill Gates on How to Stop Global Warming." *Rolling Stone*, December 9, 2010. www.rollingstone.com/politics/news/the-miracle-seeker -20101028.

44. Ferguson. *Nuclear Energy*, p. 48.

45. Science Council for Global Initiatives. "The Integral Fast Reactor." www.thesciencecouncil.com/energy-the-fast-reac tors-promise.html.

46. Office of Nuclear Energy, U.S. Department of Energy. "Gen IV Nuclear Energy Systems: Program Overview." http://nuclear.energy.gov/genIV/neGenIV1.html.

47. Quoted in Tom Avril. "The World According to Bill: Bill Gates Discusses Global Health, Electronic Privacy and His Investment in Nuclear Energy." *Investigate*, August 2010, p. 54.

48. Caldicott. *Nuclear Power Is Not the Answer*, pp. 125–26.

49. Amit Asaravala. "How Nuclear Power Works." *Wired*, July 5, 2005. www.wired.com/science/discoveries/news/2005/07/68074?currentPage=all.

50. Quoted in United Press International. "Thorium as Uranium Replacement Studied," September 13, 2012. www.upi.com/Science_News/2012/09/13/Thorium-as-uranium-replacement-studied/UPI-10481347571737.

51. Ferguson, *Nuclear Energy*, pp. 17–18.

Chapter 1: The History of Nuclear Energy

1. How did World War II help spark the development of nuclear energy?
2. What factors contributed to the nuclear power industry's growth from the 1950s through the 1970s?
3. Discuss the three incidents that have cast a cloud over the nuclear power industry.

Chapter 2: Harnessing Nuclear Energy

1. What are atoms and how are they constructed?
2. What are isotopes and how are they identified?
3. How does nuclear fission work?

Chapter 3: The Benefits of Nuclear Energy

1. Which of the nuclear energy benefits touted by supporters do you find most important? Why?
2. Which of the nuclear energy benefits touted by supporters do you find most convincing? Why?
3. Why do you think that nuclear power has more support from rank-and-file members of environmental groups than from the leadership of those groups?

Chapter 4: The Drawbacks of Nuclear Energy

1. Which argument against the use of nuclear power do you find most convincing? Why?
2. Which argument against the use of nuclear power do you find least convincing? Why?
3. Would the establishment of permanent storage facilities for nuclear waste make a big difference for the industry's future growth? Explain.

Chapter 5: Nuclear Energy in the Twenty-First Century

1. Do you think it is accurate for the nuclear power industry to call nuclear energy a "green" or "renewable" source of energy?

2. How would you and your family feel if an electric utility began building a Generation IV reactor in your community?

3. Consider your own personal stance on the issue of nuclear energy, and then explain what factor or factors would have to change for you to switch positions.

ORGANIZATIONS TO CONTACT

American Nuclear Society (ANS)
555 N. Kensington Ave.
La Grange Park, IL 60526
Phone: (800) 323-3044
Website: www.new.ans.org

The ANS is a nonprofit organization of engineers, scientists, and educators involved in the fields of nuclear science and technology. The ANS has a mandate to promote the awareness, understanding, and use of nuclear energy.

Greenpeace USA
702 H St. NW, Ste. 300
Washington, DC 20001
Phone: (202) 462-1177
Website: www.greenpeace.org/usa/en

Greenpeace is an international environmental organization that has played a leading role in the anti-nuclear movement for decades. It was initially founded in 1971 to protest nuclear testing off the coast of Alaska.

Nuclear Energy Institute
1201 F St. NW, Ste. 1100
Washington, DC 20004-1218
Phone: (202) 739-8000
Website: www.nei.org

The Nuclear Energy Institute represents various companies across the United States that are involved in the nuclear power industry. The organization works to promote nuclear energy to the American public and to encourage pro-nuclear policies at the state and federal levels.

Sierra Club

85 Second St., 2nd Fl.
San Francisco, CA 94105
Phone: (415) 977-5500
Website: www.sierraclub.org

The Sierra Club is the largest environmental group in the United States, with hundreds of thousands of members in chapters located around the country. The organization works on a wide array of pollution and wilderness conservation issues, and it consistently champions wind, solar, and other renewable energy sources over nuclear energy and fossil fuels.

Union of Concerned Scientists (UCS)

Two Brattle Square
Cambridge, MA 02138-3780
Phone: (617) 547-5552
Website: www.ucsusa.org

The UCS is an organization of scientists, teachers, and citizens dedicated to science-based solutions to global warming and other environmental problems.

Books and Articles

Fred Bortz. *Meltdown! The Nuclear Disaster in Japan and Our Energy Future*. Minneapolis, MN: Twenty-First Century, 2012. This work intended for young adults uses an explanation of the 2011 Fukushima nuclear reactor accident as the centerpiece for a wider examination of the origins and development of nuclear power.

Marshall Brain and Robert Lamb. "How Nuclear Power Works." HowStuffWorks. www.howstuffworks.com/nuclear-power.htm. This online article provides an authoritative, kid-friendly description of the basics of nuclear power generation.

Stephanie Cooke. *In Mortal Hands: A Cautionary History of the Nuclear Age*. New York: Bloomsbury USA, 2009. This general history of nuclear energy and weaponry concludes that the technology is not the answer to the world's energy and climate change problems.

Christopher Helman. "30 Under 30—the Future of Energy Is Nuclear." *Forbes*, December 17, 2012. www.forbes.com/sites /christopherhelman/2012/12/17/30-under-30-the-future-of -energy-is-nuclear. This fascinating slideshow provides brief biographies of thirty young engineers, researchers, and entrepreneurs who are shaping the future of energy—many of them by pursuing innovations in nuclear energy.

Will Mara. *The Chernobyl Disaster: Legacy and Impact on the Future of Nuclear Energy*. New York: Marshall Cavendish, 2011. This work provides a solid, understandable overview of the 1986 Chernobyl disaster and its enduring status as an antinuclear symbol.

Bill McKibben. *Eaarth: Making a Life on a Tough New Planet*. New York: Times Books/Henry Holt, 2010. One of the world's foremost global warming activists reports on the evidence that climate change has already arrived, explains how it will force wrenching changes in our ways of living, and discusses his reasons for opposing major investments in nuclear energy.

Michael Totty. "The Case for and Against Nuclear Power." *Wall Street Journal*, June 30, 2008. http://online.wsj.com/article/SB 121432182593500119.html. A concise summary of the arguments and controversies about nuclear energy.

Websites

Debate: Does the World Need Nuclear Energy? (www.ted .com/talks/debate_does_the_world_need_nuclear_energy .html). This video presented by the nonprofit organization TED presents a discussion between two prominent environmentalists with different perspectives on nuclear power and green energy—Stewart Brand and Mark Z. Jacobson.

Frontline: **Nuclear Aftershocks** (www.pbs.org/wgbh/pages /frontline/nuclear-aftershocks). This Public Broadcasting System website examines the future of the U.S. nuclear industry after the 2011 Fukushima reactor disaster in Japan.

Nuclear Energy, Nonproliferation, and Disarmament, Natural Resources Defense Council (www.nrdc.org/nuclear /default.asp). This website maintained by the Natural Resources Defense Council environmental organization provides links to a wide range of information and analysis of nuclear power and its environmental impacts in the United States and around the world.

Office of Nuclear Energy (www.ne.doe.gov). This website is maintained by the agency of the U.S. Department of Energy that is specifically devoted to nuclear power, and it provides a variety of informational resources for students, educators, and the general public.

INDEX

PICTURE CREDITS

Cover: © Kletr/Shutterstock.com
© Altrendo/Getty Images, 49
© AP Images, 21
© AP Images/Andy Wong, 68
© AP Images/Don Ryan, 77
© AP Images/Morning Sentinel, David Leaming, 65
© blickwinkel/Alamy, 45
© Cengage, Gale, 26, 38
© Claus Lunau/Bonnier Publications/Science Source, 27
© Columbia/The Kobal Collection/Art Resource, NY, 18
© Corbis, 12
© David R. Frazier/Science Source, 40
© DigitalGlobe/38 North via Getty Images, 56
© Dinodia Photos/Alamy, 67
© Jim West/Alamy, 35
© Lisa J. Goodman/Getty Images, 62
© Marie Hansen/Time & Life Pictures/Getty Images, 14
© Maxim Kniazkov/AFP/Getty Images, 58
© Medical Body Scans/Science Source, 46
© Mira/Alamy, 9
© Pallava Bagla/Corbis, 71
© Phil Degginger/Alamy, 39
© Photo Researchers, 33
© Reuters/Landov, 17, 73
© RIA Novosti/Alamy, 30
© Richard Levine/Alamy, 52
© Scott J. Ferrell/Congressional Quarterly/Getty Images, 61
© Shu Shi/Xinhua/Landov, 43
© SSPL/Getty Images, 75
© Visions of America, LLC/Alamy, 54
© ZUMA Press, Inc./Alamy, 32

ABOUT THE AUTHOR

Kevin Hillstrom is an independent scholar who has written numerous books on environmental and energy issues, U.S. politics and policy, and American history.